The Lost Boy

A search for life,
a triumph of outback spirit

Robert Wainwright

ALLEN&UNWIN

First published in 2004

Copyright © Robert Wainwright 2004

All rights reserved. No part of this book may be reproduced or transmitted in any form or by any means, electronic or mechanical, including photocopying, recording or by any information storage and retrieval system, without prior permission in writing from the publisher. The *Australian Copyright Act 1968* (the Act) allows a maximum of one chapter or 10 per cent of this book, whichever is the greater, to be photocopied by any educational institution for its educational purposes provided that the educational institution (or body that administers it) has given a remuneration notice to Copyright Agency Limited (CAL) under the Act.

Allen & Unwin
83 Alexander Street
Crows Nest NSW 2065
Australia
Phone: (61 2) 8425 0100
Fax: (61 2) 9906 2218
Email: info@allenandunwin.com
Web: www.allenandunwin.com

National Library of Australia
Cataloguing-in-Publication entry:

Wainwright, Robert, 1961- .
The lost boy : the story of Clinton Liebelt.

Includes index.
ISBN 1 74114 342 X.

1. Liebelt, Clinton, d. 1993. 2. Missing children - Northern Territory. I. Title.

363.2336099429

Set in 11/15pt Californian FB by the Typéfi Publishing System
Printed by Griffin Press, South Australia

10 9 8 7 6 5 4 3 2 1

*To my parents Rae and Arthur
and my kids
Steve, Rosie, Sean and Allegra*

1
They fell from the sky

It was raining fish outside the Dunmarra Wayside Inn. Thousands of them; tiny flapping hatchlings which appeared to have been born in the clouds above the desert and dumped into the giant parking lot built for the road trains that thundered past along the Stuart Highway.

They flopped and flailed in the puddles that formed in the rutted surface, gasping as if surprised by their abrupt entrance to life. Picked off by scavenging birds or dying as the puddles evaporated in the hot air, their existence would end almost as quickly as it began, although the stench would last for days.

Adele Liebelt watched the weird sight from inside the roadhouse. She tried to concentrate on preparing the breakfast menu chalked on the giant blackboard above her head but, like the other early morning staff, couldn't stay in the kitchen for more than a few minutes without taking another look outside.

Adele's day always began the same way—rising before dawn to open the roadhouse and prepare dozens of hot meals in time for the steady stream of travellers who needed feeding. On this overcast March morning in 1994 she had woken to the thumping sound of the torrential downpour and had been in no hurry to make the short dash between the house and the sprawling roadhouse; at least, not until she saw the fish. They had appeared from nowhere. Most were barely a centimetre long. Others were three times the size. There were even tiny crabs scuttling past the petrol bowsers. It seemed impossible.

Adele had seen many strange things during the six years she and husband Steve had lived at Dunmarra—a pinprick on the road maps of the Northern Territory; a rest place and fuelling stop for truckies, tourist buses and hire cars on the 1600-kilometre trek between Darwin and Alice Springs—but this was bizarre. She reckoned there must be a scientific answer to the phenomenon but couldn't imagine what it might be. Neither could Steve, who normally didn't rise for another hour but was dragged outside, sleepy-eyed, to see the miracle. They traced the streams of water threatening to flood the forecourt across the rain-blackened highway to a small dam beyond—the only surface water for miles—hoping it might provide an explanation. Maybe the fish had been washed from the dam—except that the roadhouse was on the higher side of the road in the otherwise flat and uninspiring landscape.

The couple's 11-year-old son, Greg, couldn't care less how they got there. He and his cousin Danniel laughed and danced and splashed their way back and forth across the driveway to see who could find the biggest fish. Greg, as usual, won the contest, just as the 6.30 a.m. northbound bus pulled in and found a space between the overnight road trains. The occupants, most shrugging off an uncomfortable night sleeping upright since the bus left Alice at 8 the night before, stumbled out, amazed at the sight.

The daily buses were not just for tourists; they also carried locals between the tiny townships dotted erratically along this loneliest of highways. But at this time of year—the end of the summer wet season when blazing daytime temperatures began to cool—the buses tended to be full of European and Japanese tourists who came to see the hostility of the Australian outback from the safety of cushioned, air-conditioned seats.

They stood, wet and staring skywards, wondering what they had walked into. In the weeks that followed the telephone at Dunmarra went mad; dozens of interviews with television and radio stations around the world all asking the same thing—why were there fish falling out of the sky in the middle of Australia?

It would remain a mystery typical of the Territory and its enduring people. Science would make some considered suggestions: that the roe, some of it perhaps dormant for more than a year, had been sucked into the air and carried to the roadhouse by the weather conditions. But where had it come from? After all, water was scarce for hundreds of kilometres in any direction and the closest beach was 1000 kilometres to the north. Had the eggs hatched in the air, or did the heavy rains which pelted the normally arid landscape trigger the process of life, and its inevitable path to death?

That was the way of things in the outback; death was a short step from anywhere in this region. Sometimes the search for answers produced nothing but more questions. Adele had tasted such a search before. She stared out past the petrol bowsers and into the forbidding, stunted bullwaddy scrub of the plains beyond the Stuart Highway to the west—remembering the events of just five months before. She watched as Greg, triumphant and prancing in the tumbling rain, inspected the first catch of fish in his short life. But Adele was thinking of her younger son, Clinton.

2
Adele

Children remember the strangest things; tiny details inside much bigger events which themselves have a profound impact on their lives. Adele could not recall much about the first nine years of her life in England, not even the day she got lost on a windswept beach in Wales and sent her family into a frenzy of panic as they searched for the slight blonde four-year-old.

But the morning her family left England for a new life in Australia would remain etched in Adele's memory. It was the tears she remembered most from the typically overcast grey day in February 1966. Her grandmother Lilian was inconsolable as two daughters, their husbands and six children boarded the Sitmar liner *Fairsky* for the six-week journey to the other side of the world. Adele's mother Patricia cried too, not so much for what she was leaving behind but for the promise of the new life ahead.

The family was close knit but had little money. Adele's father had spent 16 years in the army, stationed mostly in Singapore and Burma, where as a staff sergeant in the Royal Electrical and Mechanical Engineers he earned barely enough to make ends meet. By the time Adele was born on 4 December 1956, he was back in the United Kingdom working as a motor mechanic in the Worcestershire village of Hartlebury, deep in the English Midlands where hedgerows, elm and beech mark the gentle slopes of the fertile countryside—a stark contrast to the brutal topography of Central Australia where Adele would spend most of her life. Adele was the third child and first daughter of Victor and Patricia Stokes. There were four children in five years—brothers Glenn and Kim arrived in 1954 and 1955, and younger sister Katrina in 1958. It was far from a bleak life but there was little promise of greater comfort in the future, and like thousands of British families the Stokes became caught up in the wave of enthusiasm about migration to a new, younger and sunnier land.

It wasn't just the farewells on the Southampton docks which left an impression on Adele. Life on board the ship was memorable. The children had to go to school during the voyage. The classroom was the ship's theatre and her teacher had the longest fingernails she'd ever seen. The ship stopped in Port Said before nosing its way down the Suez Canal and through the Red Sea to Aden—one of the last ships to make the slow journey. Adele was scared of the ports in the Middle East, spooked by conversations she'd overheard about locals kidnapping little girls with blonde hair and blue eyes. Adele thought she'd be okay because she was old enough to defend herself from attack, but she worried about Katrina who was only seven.

The family arrived in Sydney on 12 March 1966 and caught the train to Brisbane where they were met by Patricia's uncles, Tom and Fred, who had moved to Australia in the 1920s and even fought under the flag of their new home in World War II. The family was taken to a migrant hostel, but the children barely had time to explore their new surroundings before their father found a job and was allocated a Housing Commission home in the burgeoning estates of the city's western suburbs.

A change of employment forced their next move, inland to Toowoomba, on the edge of the Darling Downs, when Victor Stokes got a job at the NASA tracking station built at Cooby Creek, just outside the city, for the Apollo moon mission. It was here that Adele felt the heat of the Australian landscape for the first time. The nights were often bitterly cold but the summer days could be stifling as the humidity exaggerated the average 30-degree days.

It was the water which drew Adele into her new surroundings. Like her brothers and sister she could hardly swim when the family arrived in Queensland. Their parents decided the children should be 'Australianised', and that meant learning to swim, and beach holidays. It was a time to remember—weekends at Cotton Tree on the sandy banks of the Maroochy River and holidays at Kingscliff, just across the border into northern New South Wales, with Uncle Tom, Aunt Hilda and their 10 children. The family station wagon would be packed to the gunwales with camping gear—a 12 x 12 foot tent, two sets of camping bunks (one for the girls and one for the boys), a camping sink on legs and a two-burner stove. Even the roof rack had a purpose: reshaped by Victor, it could be removed and used as a base for the double bed. The children, belying their English heritage, turned golden in the tropical sun and life was contented.

Adele's existence was again turned upside down, at the age of 14, when the tracking station closed down. Victor rejected an offer of a job at another tracking station at Carnarvon, high on the West Australian coastline, moving his family south to Victoria where he had a better paying offer as maintenance supervisor at Alcoa's Ocean Grove aluminium smelter. Her brothers would later do their apprenticeships here as boilermakers.

The move came at the wrong time for a teenager whose world, like that of most kids her age, revolved around friends and school life. The small seaside town of Ocean Grove sat at the bottom of Victoria, on the southern side of the Bellarine Peninsula south-east of Geelong, looking out onto the bleak grey waters of Bass Strait. It was the complete flipside of the warm inland climate of Toowoomba.

Adele rebelled. She hated the local school which was small compared to the high school in Toowoomba. It had crazy hours which kept them there until 4 p.m. when it was too late to go out with friends. To top it off, the school had the daggiest uniform she could have imagined—a drab grey woollen tunic totally unlike Toowoomba's bright red and navy cotton which, in hindsight, seemed to match the weather she had left behind.

There was no consoling Adele. She dropped out at the age of 15 to take a job as a shop assistant and left home two years later, moving from one communal house in town to another as she experimented with life, love and independence. She would look back in later years and wonder at the innocence of teenage life and early adulthood in the 1970s where all that mattered was fashion (satin pants and platform heels), music (Fleetwood Mac, Bob Dylan and Little River Band) and boyfriends with longer hair than their girlfriends. Her working life seemed to follow these passions. Working in a dress shop for a time, for the first time in her life Adele could spend money on new clothes rather than wearing her brothers' hand-me-down jeans. Then followed a dream job in a music store. But strong family bonds and conservative upbringing restricted the extent of Adele's rebellion. She never got drunk and, apart from smoking the odd joint, was never tempted by the cocaine and heroin she saw being offered to others around her. She was searching for a purpose to her life.

Adele's maternal grandparents, Lilian and Gerald Rose, had followed the Stokes family to Australia and also moved to Ocean Grove. They were an integral part of a childhood she regarded as so normal that it was, perversely, abnormal compared to the experiences of her friends and the people she would meet in adulthood. All she knew inside the family was love—parents who some nights would push the furniture to the edges of the lounge room and dance, grandparents who followed them to the other side of the world because they couldn't bear life without them. She had fought with her siblings and played with them even more. There was no abuse, no violence and no marriage break-ups. Nobody drank to excess. She was lucky, Adele concluded.

Life drifted by without much of a hiccup, headed nowhere in particular. Her only notion about the future was that one day she would be a wife and a mother. Her social life revolved around friends, music, mostly watching and dancing to bands at the two pubs which sat a couple of kilometres either side of Ocean Grove, at Barwon Heads and Collendia. The highlight of her teens was the night the lead singer of Little River Band, Glenn Shorrock, winked and said 'Gidday babe' as she walked past the stage. Adele was so stunned that she didn't reply.

It was on one of these nights of music that she met Graeme Corcoran, an electrician and surfie from Melbourne. Graeme was four years older than Adele—tall and nice looking, he owned a panel van to boot. When he finished his apprenticeship he moved to Ocean Grove to be closer to her. They never lived together but soon after Adele turned 21, the pair decided they needed to explore life outside rural Victoria. The broad plan was to work their way around Australia in a Kombi van. If they were still together after that they would tour the world. They roamed over the state and up through New South Wales to the Gold

Coast where Adele's brother Glenn and his wife Lu had made their home. They stayed for 10 months, working and saving for the next leg of their odyssey, through Queensland to Cape Tribulation then across the top end to the Northern Territory via Karumba. For Adele, it was the beginning of a life she could never have imagined.

3
A new life beckons

The giant termite mounds which rise randomly on either side of the Stuart Highway change colour on the drive south from Darwin to Alice Springs. The yellows and ochres of the tropical north give way to a vivid bulldust red as the ground hardens and the humidity recedes. The genius of the builders of these spindly fortresses is not immediately obvious from the window of a speeding car—both the fluted cathedral mounds rising to 4 metres in height and the smaller meridian mounds, built of digested grass, are arranged to present a knife-edge to the midday sun so their internal temperature stays around a termite-idyllic 30 degrees.

The vegetation also changes dramatically. Near Darwin the trees are tall and green, filled with birds and butterflies. Black kites chase Torresian crows across the skies, cattle wander on the road verges where signs warn of the dangers of crocodiles and water monitors. But the heavily wooded plains of the north transform to a threadbare, flat and stony landscape as the kilometres tick by in their hundreds. The outlook becomes waving fields of long pale grass broken by clumps of corkwood trees flowering in magenta, or white snow-flaked ti-tree, all framed by the distant purple of a series of ancient mountain ranges.

Though the scenery can be spellbinding it is the signs of the impossible struggle of white Australia to tame the wild outback that are most noticeable. The remains of mining and pastoral outposts, and of World War II military camps, dot the route. Pine Creek still proudly bears the signs of its gold mining heritage, as does Mataranka, its pastoral history immortalised in the novel *We of the Never Never*. Larrimah was a staging camp for 3000 servicemen on their way north to Darwin to fight and die in the jungles of Borneo and Papua New Guinea. The tiny rest stop of Daly Waters is the site of Australia's first international airfield, a refuelling depot for the early Qantas flights. The Dunmarra roadhouse marked the completion of the overland telegraph line. Newcastle Waters is a memorial to the pioneers who guided mobs of cattle across the top of the continent to the markets in Queensland. Three Ways is a road junction just north of the town of Tennant Creek where the Barkly Highway begins its trail east toward Mount Isa, through the grasslands and once-great pastoral leases of the Barkly Tablelands.

It was from Mount Isa that Adele and Graeme crossed into the Northern Territory for the first time, heading toward Alice Springs to see the wonders of Ayers Rock (recently renamed Uluru, its Aboriginal name). They stopped for the night in Tennant Creek at a rough and ready caravan park that was an obligatory facility of all towns and roadside rest stops.

Their first taste of the desert's wonders came the next day, just outside Wauchope and still 400 kilometres north of their destination. It was impossible to pass by the Devil's Marbles without stopping. The giant ball-shaped boulders scattered on either side of the highway, balanced precariously on top of each other as if about to topple and roll into the centre of the shallow valley, are believed by the local Warumungu people to be the eggs of the Rainbow Serpent.

The only stop they made on the last leg to Alice Springs was at the township of Ti Tree. Graeme noticed the police station by the side of the road and decided to avoid potential problems by registering the .22-calibre rifle he carried. Adele waited in the van, casting her eye around the dusty pit stop with its hotel and petrol station, police station and tiny school in front of a collection of tiny houses. She wondered if she could live in a place like this, an eye-blink a million miles from anywhere. Surely there had to be more to life here than what she could see. The thought passed without an answer.

They chugged into Alice Springs at nightfall, finding a camping area on Larapinta Drive on the city's western outskirts. Alice Springs was founded in 1870 as a staging point for the Overland Telegraph line. Built on the flood plains of the Todd and Charles Rivers, it nestles snugly between the hills and gorges of the Macdonnell which stretch for 400 kilometres east and west.

It was April 1979 and the tourist industry that would soon make Alice Springs an economic boom town was only in its nascent stages. Still, the city was already an automatic destination for many travellers, and there was no shortage of work, particularly as autumn turned to winter and the tourists were blown inland from the coast to the pleasantly warm and surprisingly green hinterland. They came for the raw and forbidding beauty of places like the Macdonnell Ranges which once stood higher than the Himalayas. They walked the Larapinta Trail, which stretches 250 kilometres west from Alice Springs across the range's backbone, to places like Standley Chasm where the afternoon sun glances off huge ochre cliffs, to the majesty of the gorges at Ellery, Ormiston and Serpentine and to the views from the top of Mount Sonder. The world's oldest river, the Finke, flows deep inside the Glen Helen Gorge, still crafting its path after 100 million years. It guards and feeds a valley where 12 000 red cabbage palms—the remnants of a tropical rainforest which covered the area 60 million years ago—shelter beneath the sandstone cliffs.

Watarrka National Park lies south-west of Alice Springs, at the western end of the George Gill Range. Its most famous feature is Kings Canyon, whose sandstone walls are cut like sunburned grooves and hide the fossils of marine animals embedded when the area was covered by a shallow inland sea 400 million years ago. From atop the canyon rim you can see the blur of Ayers Rock far to the south, while 300 metres below is one of the most startling visions of all—the Garden of Eden with its freshwater pool fed by splashing waterfalls and fringed by cycad palms and eucalypts. Birds—galahs, pelicans and even black swans—flock to this cool oasis.

The girth of Ayers Rock, or Uluru as it is now known, rises from the desert plains 480 kilometres south-west of Alice. Almost every rock and outcrop around the ancient monolith holds some form of symbolism for the local Anangu people, though the stories are muddled by clumsy European names. This was Adele and Graeme's ultimate destination. The weather had turned cold and windy but they still sat in awe at its base, watching the rock turn purple in the rain as waterfalls appeared magically to tumble down its grooved walls. They made the steep hike up its face, Adele fighting an earache as the temperature dropped. They wandered through the Aboriginal camps at the foot of the behemoth, sitting with elders to talk about mythology and sift through the paintings being offered for sale, but bought nothing.

It took a week to visit and wonder at everything, like Kata Tjuta to the west where a group of 30 rocks mass up to 500 metres high, polished round by the wind over millions of years. The white explorers named this place The Olgas, after the Queen of Spain, but its Aboriginal heritage runs far deeper; back to the Dreaming when it was the home of the snake Wanambi, whose hairs are the dark lines on the eastern side of the rock and whose breath is the wind which blows through the gorges. Mount Connor to the east of Ayers Rock is known by the Anangu people as Artilla, the home of men who create cold weather, who got busy that week.

The journey back to Alice Springs was cut short by the heavy rains which quickly turned the red dust into a quagmire. Adele and Graeme got as far as the Wallara Ranch Motel, the closest accommodation to Kings Canyon, when the rains set in. Owner Jimmy Cottrill, whose father cleared the first road to the canyon with axes, offered them jobs and they ended up staying for the tourist season, working as general hands in the complex.

A few months later two young constables from Alice Springs, on their fortnightly patrol along the Luritja Road, dropped in. It was a regular call-in, and the officers generally stayed the night before heading back to town. This time was no exception. One of the officers, Steve Liebelt, was immediately smitten by the tall blonde behind the counter but Adele didn't even notice him, probably because of the frantic activity around the arrival of a busload of young tourists.

Things changed that night. The motel bar was packed, music blaring as the rowdy visitors danced and drank the night away. In the middle of the noise Steve asked Adele for a dance. She accepted, much to Graeme's annoyance. It proved to be the end of one relationship and the beginning of another. His marriage already on the rocks, Steve Liebelt could not get the young woman out of his head, and she felt the same about him.

Over the next few months, Steve kept finding reasons to head back to the Wallara Ranch Motel. Graeme Corcoran was not oblivious to the interaction between his girlfriend and the big young cop but there was little he could do about it. One night Graeme presented Adele with an ultimatum: choose between him and Steve Liebelt. The next morning he packed and headed home to Victoria alone. Adele had made her choice, and a new life beckoned.

4
Steve

Steve Liebelt would always remember the smell and taste of childhood summer holidays; the days in the late sixties and early seventies when a couple of dollars could buy as much fish and chips as a bunch of hungry kids could eat, perched on the jetty at Port Elliott on the Spencer Gulf in South Australia. Dave and Mary Liebelt would often make the two-hour drive with their four kids—Steve and his three younger sisters, Mary-Anne, Jane and Susan—from the suburbs of Adelaide to the historic town where the Murray River spills into the Gulf.

But it wasn't the salt and sand of his boyhood which marked Steve for life ahead. By the age of eight or nine the youngster had already earmarked himself as a dirt-in-the-toes man, at ease in the open spaces of the Australian countryside where he lived a Huckleberry Finn existence at weekends, rabbiting in the bush, picking blackberries for Aunt Cynthia's jams and preserves, and helping Uncle Lisle milk the cows on his dairy farm at McHarg's Creek in the hills above the South Australian capital.

A suburban primary school education was followed by enrolment at the Urrbrae Agricultural High School—a sprawling complex on the city's eastern outskirts—as his parents encouraged a future in agricultural science. Steve coasted along easily in some subjects and laboured in others, preferring the limelight of the sporting arena where his towering 195-centimetre frame made him a dominant force in school athletics and even more so on the football field. It seemed that league football rather than a farming career beckoned as he neared the end of secondary education; there was little time for the dairy farm as winter weekends became a succession of matches, either for his school or the Central Districts Football Club, which drafted the raw-boned youngster at the age of 15.

At home it was a sheltered existence in a close family where Sunday school was mandatory and Friday nights were spent at the local Presbyterian church's social group. The most trouble Steve and his mates got into was being caught chucking gravel onto tin roofs around the neighbourhood late at night. Drugs were never seen, let alone dabbled with or abused, and he didn't even try alcohol until he was in his last year at high school.

The dairy industry was in downturn by the time Steve graduated and he found himself at a loss. University did not appeal and there was not enough money in professional football without an outside job. He briefly flirted with the idea of a career in the army, applying on a whim one day for a place in the officer school at Portsea. About the same time he also applied, again on impulse rather than conviction, to join the South Australian Police Force.

While he waited for acceptance to one or the other Steve went to work on a relative's horse stud where chance again threw his plans into turmoil—he fell in love with a fellow worker, Glenda Duane. The couple were married after a two-year courtship and had a child on the way when Steve was persuaded to move to Alice Springs by an offer to play football and a government job with the Federal Department of Stores. It was a turning point in his life, but also in the marriage. Central Australia was a new world for a young man breaking away from family ties for the first time—a frontier land of big ideas and big people in a town filled with big left-hand-drive cars imported by Americans working at nearby Pine Gap.

Steve ended up in the police force by association more than anything else. The Rovers Football Club seemed to have more than its fair share of the local constabulary, and when one of the district's senior officers suggested he consider a career in the police force he jumped at the chance. The pay was better than the government job, the career path clearer and he was already mates with half the cops in town. Steve still had his application in to join the South Australian force, but a year had gone by with no reply so he sat the entrance exam to join the ranks of the Northern Territory police. Oddly, he was accepted into both forces on the same day, but the choice was simple—he had crossed the border permanently and entered a brotherhood.

But there was a heavy price to pay. As much as Steve was invigorated by his new environment, Glenda came to feel increasingly isolated. Ben was born on 2 February 1978, but by the beginning of 1979 the marriage was over. Glenda took Ben back to Adelaide and Steve was on his own.

* * *

There is space to burn at Kulgera; little else, in fact. On a map, the eucalypt-fringed police station and roadhouse—Gateway to the Territory, as the signpost by the side of the Stuart highway boasts to travellers—appears to be the exact geographical centre of Australia, lying three hours south-west of Alice Springs and just above the South Australian border. The middle of nowhere has a name.

The desert wind blows hard and often. It buffets the dead flat slip of a town, whipping across the terrain from no particular direction, as if playing peekaboo with the handful of residents. The rain prefers hide and seek; unseen for most of the year while Kulgera relies on water pumped from a bore 15 kilometres away, then appearing suddenly in a torrent as if angry at being usurped by the lesser, distasteful alternative. These stormy tantrums transform the barren land with an eruption of colour from the delicate purple parakeelya flower, the wild hops whose pink petals can cure heat stroke, and the tufted poached egg daisies with their yellow centres and white silky petals.

The heat doesn't play games, however. Like an unwelcome houseguest it lounges outside on the porches, soiling the furniture and annoying those who scurry past to get inside. The petulant rains only made the heat dank as it loiters, tapping on windows, hoping to sneak into shuttered houses when the owners carelessly leave open a door or forget to turn on the air-conditioning.

Adele loved it here, almost from the moment that she arrived in June 1981 as the fiancée of a quiet and well-respected desert police officer. Steve had got the posting, normally for married men, on the promise that the couple would wed. They had already lived together for almost 18 months in Alice Springs. Now 26 and happy in her desert home, Adele was more than ready for motherhood. In an uncomplicated place like Kulgera there would be time and space to watch children grow.

Steve was the junior of the two officers stationed in the town, the police presence there expanded after the closure of the station at Finke, 150 kilometres to the north-east. He had one uniform but held two ranks—first-class constable in the Northern Territory where he had been commissioned and special constable on secondment to South Australia—because his beat straddled the two states. The 120 000 square kilometres he patrolled were covered mostly by the Simpson Desert, with little more humanity than a smattering of outpost white hamlets—the roadhouses at Kulgera, Erldunda to the north and Mount Ebenezer—as well as the two desert Aboriginal communities, Aputula and Imanpa, to the east and north-west. Steve's main policing problems centred on the Aboriginal settlements whose 500 or so residents struggled with the problems presented by alcohol and petrol sniffing.

There was also a never-ending stream of car accidents in a region of just two sealed roads and a myriad desert tracks, where speed limits were determined by the limits of the vehicle and seat belts, if fitted, were never unrolled. The verges were a graveyard of abandoned wrecks, discarded then cannibalised to keep other Frankenstein vehicles alive and running. There was an occasional firearm or drug problem and maybe a fight here and there to break up, but Constable Steve Liebelt's main duty as an officer of the law was to keep people content, however few there were.

The physical isolation suited Adele. She loved the peace and quiet. As was common along the Stuart Highway, though the town boasted only a few buildings and no more than a dozen or so permanent residents, there was no shortage of people—truckies hauling goods back and forth from Adelaide, farmers and their rowdy stockmen from surrounding cattle stations, teams of rabbiters, fighting a losing battle with a pest in the millions, and a constant stream of tourists on their way to see the natural wonders of Central Australia. When people came in from outlying stations to shop or re-license a vehicle they usually stayed for a barbecue. In most cases they stayed overnight. Hospitality was more important than clocks and deadlines.

There was always something to keep Adele busy, particularly when Steve was away on overnight trips, such as the regular patrols he made to some of the outlying cattle stations. The Police Department expected wives to fill in when their husbands were away—it was part of the deal. There were administrative duties, answering phones, dealing with tourist inquiries and the like. There was the airstrip to maintain as well as the station's generators, pumps and rescue equipment. The only duty she was paid for was keeping track of the weather. Readings had to be taken six times a day between 6 a.m. and 3 p.m. and sent by radio telephone to Darwin. Adele was paid $11 for each day's reading. (On occasions they were a guess from the roadhouse bar.)

The officer's residence was 20 years old and built of asbestos sheeting—typical of the style of home in Central Australia's small townships. It boasted evaporative air-conditioning and a large enclosed verandah on two sides, a tentative lawn and the mandatory barbecue. Although there were two bores serving the township, water supply and quality was poor. The only water fit to drink came from the rainwater tanks dotted around the complex. Medical help, the other casualty of living in the middle of nowhere, came either from the 'white box' maintained in the office or a call to the Royal Flying Doctor Service—hence the airstrip.

Life wasn't all work. There was always a party on a weekend, if not at the roadhouse then at one of the other two in the district, or even at one of the larger stations, like Victory Downs. Sometimes they would make the trip to 'town'—Alice Springs. It might mean a 500-kilometre round trip for a few drinks and a laugh but that was the norm—to a Territorian three hours in a car was the equivalent of a Sydneysider driving from Bondi to Kings Cross. But what really bonded places like Kulgera was the mateship. It was the social glue which made life acceptable in this most inhospitable of places. Acquaintanceships were the equivalent of friendships among the no-frills stationhands and truckies who made up the working contingent. Friendship meant a lifetime loyalty, in good times and especially in bad.

Steve Liebelt and Adele Stokes complied with the expectations of his superiors on 25 September 1981 in front of 100 friends and family at the Territory's only winery, Chateau Hornsby, on the outskirts of Alice Springs. The wedding was held on a Friday evening. It was no use holding it the next day, Steve decided, because it would have clashed with the Victorian Football League grand final between Carlton and Collingwood. And, as an avid Carlton fan, he wanted to watch the match with his mates before heading off on his honeymoon.

The other hot topic of conversation that day was the decision to commit Lindy Chamberlain and her husband Michael to trial over the disappearance at Ayers Rock in August 1980 of their baby Azaria. Like the rest of the nation, the community closest to the scene was divided over whether Lindy was innocent or guilty. To most, her explanation that she had seen a large dingo slinking out of their camping tent with something in its mouth seemed absurd. They had all been to Ayers Rock and camped around its base where the packs of mangy desert dogs milled around the fringes like seagulls waiting for food scraps. The scavengers were all well fed by obliging but ignorant tourists and had never been a threat to humans. Lindy Chamberlain's claimed cry of distress, 'A dingo's got my baby', was mocked rather than pitied.

As the wife of a police officer the new Mrs Liebelt found it avoided complications to not have an opinion or at least not voice it. Instead she sipped champagne and thought about what lay ahead in a life she had not contemplated in her wildest dreams until the possibility had confronted her at the Wallara Ranch Motel. Until then all she had wanted to be was a mother, or maybe a kindergarten teacher, probably in Queensland. Not that she had regrets about the turn of events since meeting Steve Liebelt. He was tall and good looking and the life of the party when the mood suited him. But he also had a quiet, reassuring presence which offered her stability and a future. Adele considered herself a careful person who took her time making decisions and she was following her heart and her head into the marriage, wherever it might lead. To others she may have appeared withdrawn, or even aloof at times, but impressions do not always reflect the truth.

Years later she would find a strange connection with Lindy Chamberlain, becoming one of the few people who empathised with the unemotional, almost chilling stoicism in front of the television cameras that so swayed public opinion against her. For now, though, there were no such complications on the horizon.

5
Parallel lives

Debbie Francksen could smell the rain as it approached from the south-west. The scent of wet dust carried on the desert breeze sent her scurrying back into her room beside the Kulgera roadhouse to change into something warmer. It had been stinking hot ever since she'd arrived in the town the week before. In fact it had barely rained since she got to the Northern Territory more than a year ago, straight from her chilly home town of Melbourne; she'd left on a whim, lured by the promise of adventure and work. Now she wondered at her decision to leave Alice Springs and come here. Another whim; this time she'd chucked in her jobs as a hospital cleaner and waitress at the Olive Tree Restaurant to follow two friends, Anita Hodge and Narda Clark, into the desert for the tourist season.

The trip had shocked her; kilometre after kilometre in the back of Anita's Honda without a signpost, let alone a town or a roadhouse. How far was this place? Debbie spent the entire trip wondering what the hell she was doing. Her fears were realised when they arrived late in the morning. A couple of early drinkers were already at the bar, sozzled, and the coffee was the pits—a lukewarm combination of instant, powdered milk and bore water. The owner, Peter Bohem, showed them to the tiny rooms they were to call home. Debbie had to share with Narda. The room didn't even have a wardrobe so they pounded nails into the flimsy walls to hang their clothes. The drone of the air-conditioner was bound to keep them awake at night, she reckoned, but at least the people seemed friendly enough. Maria, Peter's wife, put the three girls on rotating shifts: kitchen, bar and governessing her teenage brother.

The rain was falling in sheets as Debbie dashed across the forecourt and into the dining room which fronted the complex. Jumper drenched, she stood dripping in the doorway as the laughter started. With the temperature still hovering around a stifling 38 degrees, despite the rain, a Melbourne girl in a jumper in the middle of the desert stood out like a sore thumb. Debbie tried to ignore the good-natured ribbing, stripping off the offending garment and busying herself in the kitchen where they were cleaning up after the lunchtime crowd of truckies and tourists.

It was still bucketing down when she walked outside for a smoke 40 minutes later. It was much-needed rain, she guessed, judging by the way the rain bounced off the rock-hard surface. The driveway had turned into pools of red sludge as the water streamed off the corrugated iron roof to mix with spilled fuel and oil from the rows of dusty cars, utes and trucks which parked day and night out the front. The rain glistened on the fading sign which boasted the offerings inside—souvenirs, car stickers, postcards, opals and gems, groceries, fruit, meals, biscuits and batteries—and on the ice machine next to the barbecue tables.

As she smoked and stared into the grey desert Debbie sensed something amiss; a strange smell like leaking gas. She tossed the cigarette butt into the nearest puddle and rushed back inside. 'I can smell gas. There's a leak somewhere. For fuck's sake, we've got to find it before the bottle explodes and we all go up in flames.' No-one moved. Then the laughter started again. Debbie was flabbergasted. What had she done wrong this time?

Peter Bohem took her aside. It was not a gas leak but the smell of the gidgee tree, a scrubby desert acacia which grew in clumps on the other side of the highway. The dark dense wood, crafted by Aboriginals to make traditional weapons and hacked by colonial settlers to build miles of termite-proof fences, reacted chemically to the rain water: 'It's a smell you'll get to love in a place like this because it means rain, and it doesn't rain often.'

In the outback there always seemed to be a reason for a party, particularly after a rainstorm. Her blunders lingered in Debbie's mind as she joined the crowd at the bar after her shift. It was a loud affair in the tiny room, which appeared even more cramped due to its grotesque colour scheme—orange walls and green and yellow curtains. It was the characters of the customers that provided the cheer. Somehow they matched the decorations—the bobcat skin proudly displayed on the wall above the bar, the motley, curling collection of truck posters and the pinup board above the ageing jukebox covered in fading Polaroids of past happy nights. The beer and rum flowed almost as freely as the cigarettes and expletives among the knot of roadhouse workers and local stockmen. Debbie began to lose her shyness as the night wore on and joined in the raucous conversation. Mistakes forgotten, she'd become the centre of attention in a cluster of approving men when a woman she knew as Adele Liebelt walked into the room. Adele got herself a drink and joined the group, intrigued by the gregarious newcomer. Debbie had begun to tell a story about meeting a man in an Alice Springs supermarket with the largest ears she'd ever seen, 'like dinner plates'. Adele chipped in: 'Was this guy tall and skinny with a grey, balding head?' Debbie stopped, assessing the question and the questioner: 'Yes, that sounds like him. Do you know him?' Adele lit a cigarette and drew back casually as if holding the moment: 'Sure do, that's my husband's uncle. You're right about his ears.' Debbie shrank with embarrassment, her day of blunders complete.

They were complete opposites—physically and emotionally—yet Debbie and Adele hit it off immediately. Debbie was short and dark, Adele tall and blonde; Debbie was noisy and frenetic, Adele quiet and laid back. Debbie was compulsively house-proud while Adele lived in a sea of domestic disorder. Yet for all the differences, their lives were to have many parallels.

Like Adele, Debbie grew up in Victoria, although on the suburban fringes of Melbourne, and left school at the age of 16, as much out of boredom than anything else. She drifted from one menial job to another over the next few years without any real sense of direction, and with nothing much to lose, followed a friend to Alice Springs on a promise that there was plenty of work and fun on offer for young, free-spirited women. From the moment she got off the bus Debbie loved the Territory; the weather was great, the people lively and there was, as promised, an abundance of work—basic stuff like housemaiding, waitressing, cleaning and even colour-coding maps for an exploration company. The only downside was the cost of living.

Debbie found herself sharing a caravan with a couple of friends. It had all they needed—a dishwasher, TV and a microwave—but they were paying what seemed like an astonishing $100 a week for what was one of six vans in a backyard. Her move to Kulgera came largely because the lure of another adventure—this time working 'out bush'—seemed attractive.

※ ※ ※

Bernie Bliss made a bloody good rabbit stew. He'd cook it roughly but lovingly over an open fire out the back of the Kulgera pub at least once a week. He did it for Debbie and the other roadhouse girls—Narda, Sue, Heather and Diane—who counted Bernie as one of their favourite customers. They'd all sit around the fire, having a feed and drink, maybe a joint or two between them, which would be hurriedly chucked in the embers if Steve Liebelt came over after work for a sit-down. Steve was firmly anti-drugs, frowning even on marijuana.

Bernie was a rabbiter by trade; one of a handful of eccentric men who made their living gunning down the rural menace in their thousands although making little headway on their prolific numbers. Bernie was a little cleaner than most of his brethren, many of whom lived like hermits, sleeping in beaten-up caravans parked under a tree somewhere out in the bush and only coming into Kulgera every couple of weeks to get supplies and grab a bath. Though their personal hygiene might be questionable the rabbiters could all shoot the proverbial eye out of a grasshopper at 50 metres. They wouldn't get work from old Tom Cleary otherwise; the rabbits had to be head-shot so the pelts were clean enough to be sold to Akubra. Tom paid $1.50 cash for each pair of rabbits. The good shots, like Bernie, usually bagged between 60 and 100 pair a night.

Old Tom had grown up on the Nullarbor. He had earned a living from the rabbits all his life, but had lost an eye in an accident some years before and could no longer shoot. Instead he sat in his yard—outback ruddy, portly, in his mid-60s—spinning tales and drinking Fosters with anyone who happened past. He was management now; the middleman between the shooters, holding the rabbiting contract for the vast desert plains of the NT–SA borderlands. Tom and his wife Norma lived in an old railway carriage on the edge of Umbeara Station on the outskirts of town, out near the truck yards where he also held the maintenance contract. The rabbit carcasses were held in big chillers alongside the house until they could be railed to Melbourne for sale to a string of butcher shops. Norma had softened the look of the place by creating one of the few vegie gardens in the district, irrigated by the town bore conveniently located next door. She had a reputation as a great cook and convivial hostess. She abhorred alcohol but drank tea till it came out her ears.

Steve did some shooting for Tom in his spare time. He'd take out a little Suzuki 4WD some nights, careful to stay in his designated patch—south of the roadhouse as far as the South Australian border and 20 kilometres either side of Kulgera. The railway line to the east marked the border of his territory. On a good night Steve would bag 100 pairs but it was only a hobby.

There were dangers for even the most experienced. One cloudy night Steve was unable to track his way home by the Southern Cross, which usually shone so brightly in a sky filled with stars like a shattered windscreen. Normally he would be back by midnight but there was no sense taking unnecessary risks. He waited until dawn to find he was 18 kilometres from home.

When Adele fell pregnant in July 1982 her feelings were mixed. It was

※ ※ ※

her third pregnancy in two years, the first two having ended in mystifying and heartbreaking miscarriages at the end of the first trimester. The hospital tests which filled her uterus with blue dye could find no abnormalities. The only course of action seemed to be to try again.

The second miscarriage was the hardest to accept. Adele remembered the day it began with absolute clarity. She'd spent the morning in the kitchen, preparing an afternoon tea for a vice-regal dignitary who was doing an aerial tour of isolated communities in the southern part of the Territory. Commodore Johnson was due to fly into Kulgera mid-afternoon, not to the town airstrip but a slightly bigger runway 15 kilometres to the north. Steve had taken the van to meet the Commodore and bring him back for a cup of tea and quick tour before he flew back to Alice. But the pilot got mixed up.

Adele heard the sound long before it came into sight—the unmistakeable drone of twin engines as the aircraft descended, circling in search of a place to land on the sea of red below. She stepped onto the verandah, shielding her eyes from the blinding blue sky as she searched for the source of the noise. There it was; a flash of silver against the sun as it banked before final approach. No time to radio Steve. Somebody would have to be there to greet this man because that's what dignitaries expected. Adele began to run, across the hot bitumen of the highway, over the wire fence meant to stop wildlife from wandering onto the road, and through the scrubby bush that hid from view the strip of graded gravel—the airstrip—which was now a billowing cloud of dust behind the landing aircraft. She didn't give a thought to the fact that she was three months pregnant.

Commodore Johnson was already sweating by the time she arrived. The stains collected in the armpits of his white naval uniform and his brilliantly polished shoes were coated with the settling dust. He looked slightly bemused at the sight of a young woman running toward him through the bush. Steve's arrival in his four-wheel-drive, skidding to a stop alongside the plane, ended the confusion. He'd chased the plane back as soon as it was obviously headed to the smaller airstrip. Commodore Johnson was herded into the front seat. There was only room for two people. Adele turned and trudged back through the bush to make tea which was never drunk because the commodore preferred a cold beer.

The bleeding started that night. By the next day, alone and distraught, she called her mother. 'Mum, I'm bleeding, I'm bleeding again. What's happening to me? Tell me what to do,' she cried to a woman thousands of kilometres away. Patricia Stokes steeled herself: 'Put the phone down and I'll think of something.' Patricia telephoned the roadhouse and pleaded with someone to go and sit with Adele. Beyond that there was little anyone could do but hope. Three days later she miscarried.

Adele fell pregnant three months later, and breathed a sigh of relief when the first trimester passed without any problems. Maybe this time she would have the perfect pregnancy. But soon afterwards she began to bleed again. There was nothing she could do but wait, and hope. Surely this baby, too, would die. The doctors in Alice Springs had no answers. They sent her home to Kulgera where a pregnant and healthy Debbie Francksen stayed by her friend's side.

Debbie was about to be married. Soon after arriving in Kulgera she'd fallen in love with a cowboy named Bronte Bruce—a hard-bitten outback horseman who'd grown up in rural South Australia and spent his adult life on outback cattle stations either horse-breaking, shearing, mustering or fencing when he wasn't following his real passion as a saddle bronc rider on the rodeo circuit. It would always amaze Debbie how she'd fallen for a bloke like Bronte, whose stoic silence was in stark contrast to her own garrulousness, but it was a union that would stand the test of time and produce four children.

Theirs was as close as you got to a celebrity wedding in Kulgera. At least half the far-flung community were invited or decided to make the trip in from surrounding stations. Peter Bohem did not have the room to seat them all for the wedding reception so he built a new room at the back of the pub for the occasion. The setting was close to perfection; a ceremony under softening September skies, performed by Coober Pedy's Catholic priest beneath a towering brace of silver gums before an altar of railway sleepers covered in wildflowers. The romance was palpable, marred only by the short delay while the VFL grand final between Hawthorn and Essendon was completed. Somebody had forgotten to factor in the time difference between Kulgera and Melbourne. Debbie waited nervously with Adele, who was celebrating her first wedding anniversary the same day, while most of the guests, including Father Adrian Noonan, crowded into the bar to watch the game.

Christmas 1982 came and went. Adele's bleeding continued and the cramps were worsening. She was put back into Alice Springs Hospital. Still no answers except that the baby, very much alive and with two months still to go, was breech. He should be turned, and quickly. She consented, and then regretted her decision. Despite being loaded up on pethidine, she endured four excruciating hours with her legs elevated while the doctors tried without success to turn the baby. The procedure pushed her into an early labour. After two more weeks and growing doubts about whether the baby would survive, Adele demanded an emergency caesarean. She'd had enough of the bullshit and assurances that everything would be all right. She knew it wasn't. Greg was born on Australia Day 1983, six weeks early but still weighing in at 7 lb 2 oz. The shock to Adele's body was too much, doctors told her. She would never breastfeed this baby. Three weeks later—on Saint Valentine's Day—Debbie Bruce gave birth to her daughter Amanda.

6
Bush justice

The cop at the other end of the telephone was calm, considering what he was asking of Adele. The police were tracking, by air, two dangerous criminals speeding up the Stuart Highway from Adelaide toward Kulgera and needed her help to make an arrest. Could she gather all the guns and ammunition inside the police station and meet the plane which would be landing within half an hour? Oh, and they would need to take the station car as well so they could head back down the highway to intercept their target.

Adele listened in astonishment. She didn't have a clue about guns but said nothing other than she would do her best. She hung up and turned to her mother, Patricia, who was busy unpacking after arriving the previous day from Alice Springs with her daughter and newborn grandson. Adele shook her head: 'God, you wouldn't believe it. Steve's gone off on a job at Ayers Rock and his boss wants me to fill in and help arrest two armed blokes headed this way in a car.' Patricia had flown in from the Gold Coast because she wanted to lend support during the early weeks of her oldest daughter's first experience of motherhood, and already had her doubts about the outback. It was rough and hot and from what she could tell the women had to act like men if they wanted to survive. 'What sort of a place is this?' she responded angrily. 'Women should be protected, not put in harm's way. What happens if these men, whoever they are, reach Kulgera and come here to the police station? We would be defenceless.'

Adele knew her mother was right—the situation was ludicrous—but there was little she could do but comply with the request. Life in the outback threw up strange tests virtually every day. Survival meant meeting them head on, not avoiding a problem in the hope it would go away. She looked at Greg lying in his bassinet. Two days before the tiny bundle had been in a humidicrib in the Alice Springs Hospital recovering from his early, disruptive entry into the world. Today he lay in the lounge room of a desert police station, covered in a rug to ward off the icy hum of an overworked air-conditioner while the temperature outside pushed past 40 degrees. In two weeks he had already experienced the extremes of desert life.

Adele went off to find the guns and ammunition and drove out in the four-wheel-drive to meet the plane now approaching the strip across the highway. There was no time for niceties as the officers grabbed the weapons, loaded them into her vehicle and rushed off down the highway. Adele was alone again with her distraught mother, who insisted on spending the rest of the day inside the roadhouse dining room where she reckoned there would be safety in numbers. Patricia cast her eyes around the room. The two wall prints both offered dreams of mythical faraway places—one a moonscape, the other a scene of white horses splashing through a stream. The giant promotional Southwark Bitter beer can propped against a far wall and the limp indoor plants provided a sobering dose of reality. 'If the shooting starts we'll push the bassinet under the tables,' she declared.

It never did. The criminals were arrested without a shot being fired and brought back to Kulgera to be locked in the cells out the back of the main house. Patricia felt sorry for the men as she peered out the kitchen window. They looked like dogs stuck in a cage. Steve felt no such compassion. He'd got a radio call about the trouble and driven back in immediately. By the time he and the other officers returned to Kulgera with their quarry it was early evening. The officers would stay for dinner, he announced, and Peter Bohem would put them up for the night at the roadhouse. Adele shrugged and went off to cook a massive quantity of steak. The prisoners had to be fed as well—not steak of course, but black tea and sandwiches.

Patricia Stokes had gone home to Queensland when Prince Charles and his wife Princess Diana made a fleeting visit to Alice Springs a few weeks later to visit the School of the Air and climb Ayers Rock. Steve was called into Alice as part of the security team but it was Adele who was excited by the visit and wanted to go and see the royal couple on their safari. It was the only time she acknowledged her English heritage, quietly pleased when her friends insisted she resembled the shy princess.

Adele could set her watch by Greg's patterns. He went to bed on time and slept through the night, ate whatever was offered and smiled on cue. Debbie was not so lucky with Amanda, who screamed her lungs out for the first three months and refused to sleep. The two women sought each other's company even more now they were young mothers in a town with no services and thousands of miles from familial help.

Debbie had moved out to Mount Cavanagh station, south of the town, where Bronte worked as a jackaroo, but either she or Adele would make the 30-kilometre round trip to see each other several times a week. Often it was every day as Debbie would sneak down for coffee. When Steve had to be away overnight as he travelled around the district making calls to stations and roadhouses, Debbie would stay to keep Adele company because her friend hated being alone. Their friendship was more than just companionship; it was a support structure. Mothers in cities or even mid-sized country towns had access to services offering advice and even child care but, in the bush mothers could only rely on one another. Friendships were deep and for life. Adele and Debbie watched contentedly as their babies grew to toddlers; big, boofy Greg with his shock of blond ringlets and laid back nature, and petite blonde Amanda who dominated the relationship. It mirrored their mothers' friendship.

When Steve's boss Peter Guinane moved back to Darwin and Steve was promoted to officer in charge at Kulgera, it was Debbie who spent a week helping Adele move house—20 metres across the station complex from one residence to the other. It seemed ridiculous that the senior officer would have the older of the two homes with its dodgy air-conditioning, but at least the verandah was roomy, they thought.

❊ ❊ ❊

The two old foes had been needling each other all afternoon in the pub at Mount Ebenezer. It was now well into the evening and they were pissed; poking their chests out at one another like two battle-scarred elephant seals. The pub's owner, Damien Ryan, had left them alone up to now, hoping they'd give up or fall down drunk, but the battle was now becoming physical; the two of them were pushing and shoving each other as their level of bravado increased in step with the level of interest from those around them. It was becoming uncomfortable in the tiny bar, built to cater for the dozen or so locals and passing truckies but now overflowing as the crowds began arriving for the big motocross weekend. Damien hated this sort of crap. It threatened to ruin the spirit of the weekend (not to mention its financial success) during which the population of Mount Ebenezer, halfway along the Lasseter Highway between Alice Springs and Ayers Rock, jumped overnight to more than 1000.

They all came for the Radio Alice 12-Hour Enduro. It was Damien's idea really but he welcomed the sponsorship from the local commercial radio station. Dozens of the nation's top motocross riders made the trip so that for 12 hours between midnight and midday they could ride around and around a 50-kilometre off-road circuit carved each year out of the bush at the back of the roadhouse. The crowds loved it and there was a $5000 first prize for the riders. The last thing Damien needed was a punch-up.

First-class constable Steve Liebelt, in town to keep a professional eye on proceedings, had been watching from the other end of the bar. It was his job to take the sting out of moments just like this, before things got out of hand. He pushed his way through the knot of drinkers, grabbed the two protagonists by their collars and dragged them to the door.

'Now don't anyone follow me. Just get on with your drinks. I'm taking these two outside so they can get on with it in peace,' he warned as a hush came over the room.

As owner of the pub, Damien followed him outside where Steve had squared the two against the wooden-slatted wall and was laying down the law—Northern Territory-style. 'You blokes can punch the shit out of each other for all I care. Just do it out here; not on the lawn but over the other side of the road. Any closer and I'll have both of you.'

The men, sobered momentarily by the intrusion of the big copper, shuffled off obediently. Steve and Damien stood on the verandah, watching as they resumed their argument. Within seconds one took a swing and they both tumbled onto the verge, doing more damage by rolling on the gravel than by the blows they landed. Satisfied, Steve turned back to go inside. 'Mate, all you have to do is take away their comfort—the audience and a bit of lawn. They'll be back inside in a minute, with a bit of bark missing, but I'm sure they'll be a bit quieter.'

That was the way policing was enforced in the Territory, with a flexibility that carefully bent the law to maintain order, and Steve Liebelt was better than most at administering bush justice. The big man was prepared to give a bloke a clip behind the ear as a warning rather than make an arrest. It was often all that was needed to put out the fire in the belly of a rum-soaked stockman, and more times than not Steve reckoned he made the right choice.

But there were times when he underestimated his foe. Maria Bohem rang one day in a panic. A young woman had just staggered into the roadhouse screaming for help, claiming she had been kidnapped in her own car and been forced to drive south from Alice Springs. Inconsolable, she managed to tell how the kidnapper had got into her car as she sat at a stop sign, jammed what she thought was a gun (and later turned out to be a piece of dowel) into her ribs and demanded that she drive to Adelaide. She spent the best part of three hours sobbing at the wheel as she sped down the Stuart Highway against her will. Forced to stop at Kulgera to get petrol, she made a run for it. The kidnapper, a young man with a long record of violence, sped off in the car, still heading south.

Steve and his new offsider, Constable Bruce Hoskings, went off in pursuit. They soon caught up with the alleged kidnapper and ran him off the road. It was the start of their troubles. Steve later related the story, which became part of local folklore.

'This young bloke got out of the car. He was just a little fella but he was very excitable and wanted to pull me on.

'I said to him: "Look mate, we don't have to do this; not out here. Just make it easy on all of us." Before I knew it he'd broken my nose. I didn't even see it coming. I said: "No, no, no. Now why in the hell did you do that?" He was still dancing, pleased with what he'd done: "Come on mate. I've killed bigger pricks than you."

'My offsider was opening the door of the wagon to put him inside and didn't see a thing. The first he was aware of it was seeing me using the upper part of the little bastard's body as a battering ram to get him in the back. He wouldn't stop. The wagon was rocking all the way back to Kulgera. By the time we got him back to the station it was late afternoon and too late to get him all the way to Alice Springs so we put him in the cells for the night. The next morning we backed the wagon up to the back of the cells to load him up.

'I said to him: "Come on mate; in ya hop." He looked at me: "If you want me then come in here and get me." So we had another roustabout in the cells. I mean, this bloke could go hammer and tongs but we finally got him in the back of the wagon.

'But that wasn't the end of it. He rocked the wagon all the way to Erldunda Station and by the time we got there I'd had enough; I mean, we still had 200 kilometres to go before we got to Alice. I drove in there, borrowed a blanket which I put in the front seat next to Bruce. Then I put the fire hose on him. Can you imagine sitting in the back of a flooded paddy wagon, dripping wet in the middle of winter? It shut him up.

'We got about 30 kays out of Erldunda and I stopped again and walked around the back. I said: "How you doing in there now mate?" He was shivering like shit, curled up in a bundle: "It's bloody cold in here," he said. I knew I had him then: "I'll tell you what. I'll give you a blanket if you'll pull your head in. Then we'll get on fine."

'We had no trouble for the rest of the trip. Everything went well until we got to the lockup at Alice. The blokes saw us come in; me with a black eye and my nose spread across one side of my face bringing in this bloke half my size. They all started laughing at me. I handed him over and left. I heard later that he decked two coppers before they knew what hit 'em. He could fight, that boy. Turns out he'd been a golden gloves fighter for eight or nine years and boxed in one of those travelling tents.'

There were many facets to being an outback cop, as many out of the distinctive olive green uniform as in it. Successful policing meant pitching in and becoming an authoritative but sympathetic cog in the workings of a community that barely numbered one person for every 500 square kilometres. There were times that his patrols took Steve as far as Coober Pedy, almost 700 kilometres across the border into South

Australia. On other days he would make a 500-kilometre round trip to a remote cattle station just to re-license a couple of trucks or firearms for the owner or his workers. On Thursdays and Saturdays he would act as an ex-officio stock inspector down at the cattle yards when station owners from all points of the compass trucked in their cattle to load them on trains headed to southern markets. Train days were as much a social gathering as anything and Steve would end up helping to first unload and load the beasts, sometimes numbering 1000 or even 1500 head, onto the rail carriages. The cold beer slugged back sitting in the dust of the stockyards afterwards was welcome but never seemed to slake the thirst from a hard day's work. Many times he ended up hosting an overnight barbecue when the visiting officers' quarters at the back of the complex became a place for stockmen to sleep off the booze before heading back to their stations the next morning.

Every few years, the dozen or so police whose jurisdictions covered the borders of the fearsome Simpson Desert got together to trade war stories about what they called 'real policing'. The officers at Kulgera, Birdsville, Oodnadatta and Coober Pedy were separated by thousands of kilometres and three state borders yet their professional duties, issues and problems bore a common thread. What the rule book didn't cover was answered by a combination of common sense and a genuine understanding of their communities.

They met in the red sand dunes of Dalhousie Springs; an oasis of artesian springs 350 kilometres west of Birdsville in one of the driest parts of the continent. The springs are the focal point of what would become the Witjira National Park—almost 8000 square kilometres of dunes, stony tablelands and floodplain which once formed the Mount Dare pastoral lease. The ruins of the old homestead were all that remained of European incursion in a land that for thousands of years beforehand had provided water, shelter, food and medicines for the Arrernte, Wangkangurru, Arabunna and Luritja peoples. The ancient springs also had mythological significance.

There were no comfortable hotel rooms for hundreds of kilometres and nowhere to buy a good steak or a cold beer. Instead, Steve and his colleagues camped in the middle of this arid region they were tasked to patrol, reliving searches they had launched to find those who had entered the Simpson and not found their way to the other side. Some were tourists, blithely unaware of the potentially fatal consequences of such a journey. Another was a group of geologists, used to living in the open for days at a time but still at risk if something went wrong. On one occasion they launched a massive aerial search for an experienced cameleer who had broken radio contact. When he was found two days later heading toward Birdsville the man, his ego bruised that such a fuss had been made, insisted he was not lost, he just had radio problems. Nevertheless, the incident only emphasised the dangers of the desert and the pivotal and obligatory role that Steve and his colleagues played in protecting those who ventured into its depths.

As the dusk beckoned one night, with the beer and stories flowing freely, they hoisted one of their number—a police pilot who happened to play the bagpipes—on top of a four-wheel-drive and turned on the rotating blue lights. With an eerie mist drifting off the warm springs and the squall of the bagpipes shattering the evening silence, it seemed to the laughing men that they could be standing alongside Loch Ness in Scotland.

7
42 wheels

Douglas Crabbe drained the last mouthful of his coffee and banged in on the bar. 'Another one of these, love, and don't forget the Bundy nip,' he slurred, shoving the empty mug toward Debbie Bruce.

Debbie ignored the comment and walked back into the kitchen to get a fresh mug, not that the rude bastard deserved one. He was obviously drunk. Who knew how many rum-soaked coffees he'd had that evening. At the bar she added a measure of rum and passed the mug over: 'That'll be $2.' Coffee was free for truckies at the roadhouses but the rum was extra.

'Whaddyamean. I bin sitting 'ere all night drinkin' it for nuthin', and now ya wanna charge me. Get fucked.' The other barmaid, Heather, had avoided intimidation earlier by not charging for the nip. Now she was off and Debbie had taken over to work the night shift from 8 p.m. to dawn. She wasn't intimidated though she was a bit wary of the truck driver known as Crabby. He had a reputation for being sullen and having a quick, explosive temper. Adele and others had had similar experiences with him: 'Don't argue, Crabby. You know the rules. You can't expect to get the rum for nothing. Heather did the wrong thing. Pay up.'

Crabbe glared. He knew she was no pushover and that he would have been in trouble if her husband Bronte was in the bar, but Bronte wasn't there. 'I told you I'm not payin' for this sort of shit. You can fuck off.' He threw the coffee at her, smashed the mug on the bar and stormed out. It was the last Kulgera would see of Douglas Crabbe. Debbie Bruce would later look back on the incident and realise just how lucky she had been.

Crabbe was, by his own admission, prone to irrational and impulsive behaviour that, coupled with alcohol and drugs, could lead to a sudden, dangerous explosion of rage. For this he was regarded as an exception amongst the rough and ready but affable breed who plied the lonely highways of the interior. Crabbe drove for Northern Transport out of Adelaide, working the route to Alice Springs and Darwin where he delivered mainly fuel and general goods. He was a regular at the roadhouses which dot the main highway, serving as lighthouses for comfort, sleep, food and a cold beer. Crabbe was accepted but his demeanour and temper set him apart as a man to be tolerated rather than embraced by the generally accepting social network. It was like treading on glass. If the booze didn't set him off in a verbal and sometimes physical tirade of abuse then Crabbe was often off his face on the cocktail of drugs that he and most of his road brethren guzzled to keep them functioning to drive the thousands of tedious kilometres expected each working week.

Crabbe's problems came to an abrupt and tragic climax one night in August 1983, not long after his confrontation with Debbie Bruce. Crabbe was at Ayers Rock when his temper ignited, leading to an infamous crime that once again placed the Northern Territory in the international headlines for all the wrong reasons. He had been drinking for some hours at the Inland, one of the ramshackle roadside motels, and getting progressively more irritable and abusive. When the staff decided they'd had enough and booted him out, humiliated, drunk and apparently drug-crazed, Crabbe got into his truck and drove a short way down the road. Unhooking his trailers, the angry madman then turned his prime mover around and aimed it at the front wall of the motel, smashing into the crowded bar and killing five people and injuring another 20. To compound his heinous act, Crabbe ran off. There was just the one nursing sister, who operated the local health clinic, to deal with the carnage until help arrived from Alice Springs.

Steve Liebelt got a call just after midnight. Ayers Rock was not in his jurisdiction but the divisional inspector, Bryce Fardhall, who was staying overnight, was needed at the scene to coordinate the search for Crabbe. Steve went with him on the five-hour dash. They arrived just after dawn to the scene of devastation and the angry search for Crabbe who had fled into the bush.

At his subsequent trial, Crabbe pleaded temporary insanity. He claimed he didn't know what he was doing and had no memory of the incident or the deliberate actions he took to first protect his load and then ram the flimsy building that the owners would later rebuild in defiance of the wanton destruction.

By chance, two famous writers were in the crowded courtroom. The British authors Salman Rushdie and Bruce Chatwin had travelled together to Alice Springs to research Chatwin's latest book, *The Song Lines*. Some years later, at a literary memorial to Chatwin after his death, Rushdie would recall the experience, and Crabbe's defence:

> At the Inland Motel near Ayers Rock we hear about the truck driver, Douglas Crabbe, who was thrown out of the pub one night and went outside and drove his truck into the bar, killing and maiming a number of people. The locals rebuilt the pub, even though they knew the whole motel was going to be demolished a year later anyway. Later we are in Alice Springs and hear that Crabbe's trial is under way and he is in the witness box. Bruce and I grab our notepads and go off to play court reporter. Crabbe is softly spoken, dapper, with a little brown moustache and button-down blue shirt with dark blue knitted tie. While giving evidence he keeps his eyes cast down. His line is that he didn't know what he was doing, he has no memory of it: a temporary insanity plea, I suppose. He says repeatedly that he's not the sort of man to commit such a crime. When pressed about this, he says: 'I've been driving trucks now for 4½, and treating them as if they were my own.' (He doesn't quite add 'children'.) 'So for me to half destroy a truck is completely against my personality.' I look at the jury and see them all begin to sort of hiss and grind their teeth and decide to send him away and throw away the key. Afterwards I say to Bruce: 'Wasn't that an amazing piece of self-destruction?' Bruce is genuinely puzzled, betraying an unexpected innocence. 'I don't see what was so wrong with

that. He was actually telling the whole truth about himself. He was being honest.'

Crabbe expanded on the story at his appeal against the life sentence, insisting he had been suffering a psychotic episode, brought on by a long-time drug addiction combined with alcohol and fatigue, and that his actions were independent of his will, his mind and body being in a state of automatism. A supporting statement from another truckie said that 'overtiredness, alcohol, pep pills and frustration can cause acts that are totally foreign to normal behaviour and not remembering what you did is a common occurrence'. Crabbe lost his appeal.

Australian rock band Hunters and Collectors would immortalise the tragedy in their anthem '42 Wheels'.

* * *

You could generally pass the Kulgera gymkhana grounds along the road to Finke without giving it a second thought. But once a year the dusty paddock, with its old tin shed and rustic toilet block, was transformed into the venue for the biggest event on the local social calendar, the Kulgera Gymkhana and Ball, held on the Father's Day weekend in September.

It was a time when the district population was drawn together from the scattered stations in a celebration of optimism that defied their surroundings and grafting lifestyles. The crowd, some from as far away as the opal fields of Coober Pedy, 700 kilometres to the south, would begin gathering on the Friday evening, turning the roadhouse and its surrounds into a giant camping ground awash with people, horses and dogs.

The gymkhana itself was held on the Saturday; a fun but nonetheless serious test of horsemanship in a country where the horse ranked second only to the four-wheel-drive. Riders and their mounts took on a program of barrel races, tent pegging, camp drafting and even a night horse event just after dusk, before the inevitable country and western band struck up for the night of dancing ahead. Like horsemanship, dancing was a serious business and the old tin shed, a furnace in the heat of the day, took on different, carefree perspective under lights. It was here in 1983 that Adele and Debbie met Candy Smith, another young woman who'd found her way into Central Australia from the relative comfort of the coastal cities.

Candy was fresh from teacher training college in Adelaide when on the spur of the moment she accepted a position as governess at Allambie Station, south-east of Alice Springs. A young woman unsure of what life held and with no particular ambition beyond settling down one day to have a family, her childhood spent roaming the Adelaide Hills, keeping goats in the backyard of the family's four-acre property, had not prepared her for the savage truths of station life in the outback. She spent her first few frightened nights, including her 21st birthday, lying awake listening to the dingoes howl in the desert beyond her tiny room, at the back of the shed which housed the mustering plane. At dinner she watched out the window in naive horror as the owner's blue heeler enthusiastically tore apart the head of a steer killed a few hours earlier to put fresh meat on the table. Meat was something you bought, already packaged, in a supermarket or wrapped by the butcher, not killed out the back while the potatoes were boiling. Despite the shock she never once regretted the adventure, nor the life of a governess, which only confirmed her own desire to have a family of her own.

It was here that Candy caught the eye of Peter Kerr, or rather, he caught her eye. She had just returned from a holiday at home in Adelaide to find all the men were out on a mustering camp and had accompanied her employer's wife out to the camp to take food to the men. The nights were turning cold, and as they approached the camp just after dusk she could see the men huddled around a big fire, rugged up in coats and hats. One ringer stood out from the others; Peter Kerr stood slightly to one side, tall, lean and with a flourishing moustache visible beneath the brim of his hat. Candy thought he was the sexiest man alive. So did many of the other young women in communities from Alice Springs out to Kulgera where Peter had a reputation as a larrikin and a bit of a ladies' man. Adele and Steve already knew Peter well. He used to stay with them when he was working as a stock agent for Elders and Dalgety's, making trips to Kulgera to supervise the cattle loading at the rail siding on the edge of town. They were taken aback when Peter introduced

Candy to them as his girlfriend at the Kulgera Ball, not because he had an attractive woman on his arm but because he described her in such a specific fashion. The Kulgera gymkhana grounds held a special place in Peter Kerr's life. He had held a party for his 21st birthday in the old tin shed, and now he was introducing the woman who would become his wife to his best mate.

The only time Peter had spent out of the Territory in his life was the few years he studied at an agricultural college in Queensland. He had grown up in Alice Springs where his stepfather was a builder and his mother worked as a journalist with the local ABC radio. Peter's interest in cattle had stemmed from holidays spent at the Lucy Creek Station 200 kilometres out of town where he fell in love with the Australian bush. Life seemed uncomplicated out in the open and he set his sights on becoming a jackaroo, which proved a stepping stone to the more lucrative career of stock inspector.

Steve Liebelt had met Peter a few days before he was due to marry Adele. The pair had hit it off immediately and Peter was invited to the wedding at the last minute. They saw themselves in each other—cocky young men, likeable pranksters who rolled with life's punches and were the life of any party—but the mutual respect went a lot deeper.

Peter was amazed at the way others gravitated to Steve when they needed help. It wasn't just his size which made people notice him as he walked into a room but something in his manner, which was secure and comforting. He watched time and again as people sought out Steve to talk about their troubles. And he never once turned anyone away.

The same went for his skills as a copper. Peter had watched his mate's diplomacy in amazement some nights at the Kulgera pub as Steve managed to talk some pissed ringer out of trying to fight everyone. It wasn't that the big fella was soft; quite the opposite. He had also seen the brute strength of the man as he grabbed some bloke by the shoulders and shoved his head straight through the fibro wall. Steve Liebelt was tough when he had to be. There was no mucking around if someone was messing with him, but he always tried the quiet option first, sometimes even taking off the police uniform and having a drink with a potential troublemaker. As a figure of authority Steve had to lead with a fairly firm hand, always mindful that the people you were trying to control were those you might also have to rely on at some stage. Many of the men who lived and worked around places like Kulgera worked flat out for three or four weeks at a time—16-hour days without a break to get a mob of cattle out of a paddock in the bush and onto the train bound for Melbourne. When they came into Kulgera for a beer you had to give them some latitude. It was a question of degree, and Steve Liebelt managed it better than most.

Steve was Peter Kerr's best man when he married Candy a few months after the Finke Ball. Though she and Peter would live mostly on cattle stations or in Alice Springs, Candy slipped comfortably into the network of friendships among the young women of Kulgera. The two couple's lives, which had followed similar paths as they arrived and settled in the district, now continued into the next phase of adulthood—becoming parents.

Adele wanted a second child and fell pregnant in June 1984. It was a nervous wait to see if she would escape the bleeding which had accompanied the first three pregnancies but this time she didn't even get morning sickness. In the meantime there was something of a baby boom. Debbie Bruce had also fallen pregnant and Candy made it a threesome soon afterward, followed by Narda, who had left Kulgera to work at Victory Downs station out toward Ayers Rock, where she met and married the owner, Bruce Morton. Adele and Narda would have sons—Clinton and Matthew—while Debbie and Candy would have daughters—Melissa and Jacquie.

※ ※ ※

The twisted, buckled remains of the once clean white Range Rover shattered the image of its former opulence, just as the accident had shattered the lives of those inside when it rolled on the uneven verge of the partly-sealed desert highway. Nobody would ever know what caused the driver to lose control—a sudden swerve to avoid an animal perhaps, or the blinding light of the midday sun. More likely it was just the inexperience and naivety of a city driver in the outback. Not that it mattered because the tragic result was the same—a dead woman and er husband in a coma with critical injuries. He might or might not survive.

These jobs were the bad times of desert policing, Steve Liebelt thought as he surveyed the wreck, lying by the side of the Stuart Highway 50 kilometres south of Kulgera. In the three hours since a traumatised motorist had rushed into the police station with news of the accident a Royal Flying Doctor crew had been sent from Alice Springs to collect the injured man and the body of his wife. Steve had been left with the task of getting the car's remains back to the police compound at Kulgera and writing his sad but necessarily objective report.

But there was something not quite right. He and Bruce Hoskings had searched the car for other survivors when they arrived at the scene but found no-one. There was nothing in the back but camera equipment and personal items in upturned suitcases—and a pile of baby clothes. Baby clothes and no baby? It didn't make sense. They searched again. Still nothing. Now the gore was gone Steve wanted to have another look, just to make sure. As he poked through the back of the car he heard the sound; a smothered whimpering from somewhere down near the floor, under what was left of the front seat. He pulled aside what looked like a basket (it was in fact an upturned baby carrier) and there it was—a baby, weeping softly as if it knew what had just happened.

Steve froze in shocked excitement. He had just witnessed a miracle: 'Shit, Bruce, there *is* a baby here; I fucking knew it. I think it's a boy and he's okay, not even injured.'

Bruce had been on the radio, getting an ETA on the truck they needed to hoist the wreck and get it back to Kulgera. He contacted the flying doctor pilot but it was too late for the plane to turn back on its way to Alice Springs. They would have to care for the child for several hours until the plane could return.

Adele heard the men outside the front window, the urgency in their discussion, and knew something was seriously wrong. She opened the door to find Steve holding a dirty bundle in his arms. He was succinct: 'Can you look after this baby, Adele? The mother's been killed and the father's badly injured. I've got to get back out there. Get Wendy over to give you a hand.'

Wendy, Bruce Hosking's wife, was nursing her own newborn child. Putting aside the emotion of their task, the two women bathed the infant which they guessed was probably only three or four months old.

The warm water comforted him a little but he was hungry and tired. Even so, he rejected the bottle of formula that Adele offered. It was clear he had been breast-fed. There was only one course of action and without hesitation Wendy offered the baby her breast. He took it, tentatively. Adele and Wendy burst out crying as they watched him. Occasionally he would stop and look up at Wendy, as if questioning why he was feeding from a strange woman. Twenty minutes later, mercifully, he dropped off to sleep.

8
'Clinger'

Clinton Victor Liebelt was born on 12 February, 1985 at the Alamanda Private Hospital in Southport on the Queensland Gold Coast. Adele chose the birth date—two weeks premature—because after so many bad experiences with pregnancy she wanted to feel that for once she was in control. There was no medical reason to feel insecure. The pregnancy had been almost perfect, with no sign of the bleeding that had plagued her previously. She didn't even have morning sickness but Adele was still wary, suspicious that something could go terribly wrong.

Steve had four months' holidays owing so the couple decided to move temporarily to Queensland so Adele could be close to her parents and siblings when the baby was born. Like most Territorians, which she now firmly considered herself to be, Adele didn't feel isolated in her daily life but the sheer physical barrier of distance emphasised just how far she was from her family. It was the one aspect of desert life that was difficult to accept for people not born and raised in the Northern Territory. She remembered how her grandmother felt on the docks that day in 1966 when the family she had loved and raised were travelling to the other side of the world. Daily telephone calls aside, it was just as bad for Patricia Stokes who silently questioned her oldest daughter's decision to live in Central Australia, among its natural dangers and a machoistic culture she abhorred. It was not the life she would choose and Patricia felt disconnected from what she considered a strange and tough existence, even more so now there were grandchildren whom she would rarely see.

A visit to an obstetrician soon after settling into her parents' home confirmed Adele's fears that all was not as perfect as it appeared. The baby was healthy but lying in a transverse position. The doctor was confident there was still time to turn the baby gently into the correct position and prepare for a natural birth but Adele, remembering how the manoeuvre had not worked with Greg, was not convinced. It made little difference to her how the baby came into the world as long as it arrived safely. She opted for a caesarean section. The doctor offered two dates for the delivery, the 12th or the 19th. Adele chose the 12th because her mother's birthday was the 19th.

The pre-med made Adele groggy but she was conscious as she was wheeled into the theatre. As she waited for the anaesthetist to knock her out, Adele confirmed in her mind two difficult decisions. The first was for herself; she'd had enough children and would have her tubes tied. Besides, Steve already had another child, Ben, from his first marriage. The family was big enough. Neither the doctor's protestations about a woman under 30 making such a decision nor her mother's concerns about the timing of the operation would dissuade her. The second decision was for Greg. Her inability to breastfeed him weighed heavily on her conscience. Like most mothers in the warmth of their first pregnancy Adele had wanted perfection. Reality had changed that perspective and she would not breastfeed Clinton because that seemed to be unfair; what was good for one was good for the other. She had made her position clear to the nursing staff and didn't want to be pestered.

Adele woke up in some pain as the orderlies wheeled her back to the ward. She smiled as they confirmed her intuition that the baby was a boy but when the nursing staff brought in the healthy 7 lb 4 oz infant a few minutes later, he was not as she'd expected. Clinton had black hair, not the fine blond down of Greg, and his skin was marked with red as if somebody had been leaning on him. It was a momentary pause caused by expectation rather than disappointment. She looked again, this time through the eyes of a new mother, and saw the second son she desperately wanted. He was perfect—tiny, quiet and wrapped tightly in the hospital-issued checked bunny rug. Greg was beside himself with excitement about 'Clinger' and offered the baby his most prized possession—a soiled satin pillow he called Ninny. The brothers had bonded.

The lights went out the first night Adele brought Clinton home to his grandparent's two-bedroom mobile house on the banks of the Nerang River. It happened again on the second night, and the third, and the fourth, as Queensland Premier Joh Bjelke-Petersen and the trade union movement embarked on their eight-month struggle using basic services as a political football. So this was life in the city—20 minutes of light followed by an hour of darkness night after night, and angry citizens listening to radio stations to find where they could buy candles. The water in Kulgera might be far from pure but at least the power supply was endless and secure.

Adele and Steve headed home two weeks later, via Adelaide, to see Steve's family. Their arrival at Kulgera was a nightmare. In the months they had been away a plague of mice had raced through three states. A mild winter the previous year had extended the breeding season and a long, dry autumn had increased the food supply in abundant grain crops across southern Australia. The result was devastating as the population explosion swept through Western Australia, South Australia and upwards to the Northern Territory. They got as far as Kulgera, and the Liebelt home. There were dead mice and mouse shit everywhere. They had nested in the linen cupboard and the clothes drawers, eaten their way through the kitchen and died in the wall cavities. The house stank. It would take three days to clean it out and save what they could of their possessions.

※ ※ ※

He was her little atom; a frenetic bundle of energy who refused to stop exploring his expanding world until late at night after what seemed to be hours of gentle coaxing and rocking. Eventually Clinton would collapse into a restless slumber but it never lasted more than a few hours—a portent to the restless enthusiasm that would mark his character. Her last night in the Alamanda Private Hospital in Southport was the last full night's rest Adele could remember. Clinton was happy and healthy, eating solids within 12 weeks, but he would not sleep. The other babies—Debbie's daughter Melissa and Candy's daughter Jacquie—slowly extended their sleeping hours as they grew to energetic toddlers, but not Clinton. Despite his difficult start in life Greg had been an easy baby, and Adele had not experienced the nightmare of sleep deprivation. It was debilitating. Even daytime sleeps were abandoned for a boy who refused to close his eyes while he had the energy to keep them open. Seven o'clock was bedtime for the boys. Greg accepted his fate, even longed for it, but Clinton would lie in his bed and scream; great gulping sobs that could not be ignored for more than a few minutes. Visits to paediatricians in Alice Springs offered little respite. Controlled crying was the only way, they said to Adele. Don't give in to the demands and he will eventually teach himself to go to sleep. It didn't work, and neither did drugs like Phenergan. Letting him sleep in her bed was the only way he'd go to sleep.

Apart from the problem of Clinton's wakefulness, Adele revelled in life with her young family. The boys were rarely sick, apart from the usual colds. The Flying Doctor Service made frequent visits, when all the babies in the area would be weighed, measured and given their inoculations. Supplies were easy to get. They held a bush order account at Coles in Alice Springs. Adele would telephone every few weeks with an order and the food would be transported down the next day on a bus. The only thing they missed out on was fresh milk. There was no television reception, but they had a video player fed by a steady stream of *Sesame Street* and *Play School* tapes sent from Queensland by Patricia Stokes.

Contact with other children was not difficult. Adele would simply take the boys to Alice Springs for a few days, or visit other mothers on nearby stations. The women even established a network of hand-me-down clothes. It was a circle of communication and understanding as much as anything else; enhancing the sense that life in the outback relied on friendships and support.

There were constant reminders of the hazards of desert life. Every few months, and inevitably without warning, Kulgera was struck by a sudden and blinding whirlpool of sand. It was destructive if a house was left open and frightening if you were caught in one out in the open, as Adele and the boys found one day when they were trapped halfway between the house and the roadhouse as a thick red cloud rolled across the plains toward them. In the few minutes it took to run with pram and toddler to the house they were surrounded by vicious swirling sands that cut visibility to a few metres. The race to tape down the windows came too late; the rooms were already inches thick in desert dust. In an occurrence equally frightening, the station complex flooded once, forcing Adele to abandon the house and wade half a kilometre through thigh-high muddy waters carrying a baby to reach the safety of the roadhouse, which stood on slightly higher ground.

* * *

Every police station in the Northern Territory had at least one Aboriginal tracker, paid and housed at the complex against the day the police needed a guide to search the deserts they knew so well. Kulgera's tracker was Brownie Doolan, a member of the Aputula people, born near Finke 60 or even 70 years before—nobody could ever find out exactly when. Brownie had lost count, and it hardly mattered. He did little tracking—though Steve reckoned he could track a fly up a wall—but contented himself gardening and doing odd jobs around the police complex where he had a little house and lived with his wife, Violet. Their kids had long grown up and scattered but Brownie had a soft spot for young Greg Liebelt. Greg would follow Brownie around the grounds with his little plastic wheelbarrow, copying the gentle, quiet tracker as he tended what little garden there was. He built Greg a sandpit under the water tank and perched on the side drawing marks in the red sand to teach his inquisitive young student the art of tracking. Whenever Adele approached the marks were hurriedly erased. This was men's business, she was chided by Greg.

Brownie eventually retired and moved back to settlement life out in the desert near Finke. Some years later Adele heard that he had been taken to Alice Springs hospital suffering from acute appendicitis. She took the boys to see the old tracker but didn't recognise him among the men wearing pyjamas on the ward until he turned and grinned, 'Hello missus.' Adele realised she had never seen him without his hat.

Brownie was very much a traditional desert dweller, heading out into the bush every few weeks to kill a kangaroo. He'd hang the carcass in the toilet of his little house and slice off a piece whenever he wanted to eat, always cooking over an open fire outside. The kitchen was never used. At one stage the Police Department decided its trackers should have fridges in their homes, so Steve dutifully drove to Alice Springs to buy a fridge for Brownie. He set it up in the house, turned it on and presented it to the old man.

'There you are; now you've got a fridge,' he said.

'But Boss. What do I need this for?' Brownie replied, puzzled.

Steve went over to the house and got a water jug. He filled it up and put it in the fridge. 'There. Now you'll always have cold water.'

It was the only thing Brownie ever put in his fridge.

※ ※ ※

Toward the end of 1985 there was a growing sense that the couple's time in the town was coming to an end. In order to move to Kulgera in the first place, Steve had passed his exam to become a first-class constable. He passed his sergeant's exam in 1984 to become officer-in-charge when Peter Guinane moved on, and now he was looking for an opportunity to win the rank officially. That meant leaving Kulgera, probably moving back to Alice Springs. It seemed to Adele that they would somehow end up in a place like Darwin as the career of her husband, encouraged by his superiors, sauntered ever upwards. Easy-going, dependable and likeable, he was a big man (standing somewhere around the old six foot, five inch mark) in a land where strength and presence was respected. In January 1986 the opportunity presented itself when a vacancy was created back in Alice Springs. After five years in a township barely 500 metres long and 50 metres wide, it was time for Steve, Adele and their two boys to move back to the town.

9
'What's the sea, Mummy?'

God apparently told tattooed Englishman David Brett to travel halfway around the world to Australia, climb Ayers Rock and be transported to heaven. It was 26 January 1986—Greg Liebelt's third birthday—when the delusional tourist was last seen climbing an area away from the marked path toward the summit. The discovery of his body created headlines around the world, but not because of his own sad demise. A few metres from where he fell to his death that day a park ranger noticed the remains of a piece of clothing sticking out of the dirt. It was identified as Azaria Chamberlain's matinee jacket, bloodied and torn—near the mouth of a dingo's den.

A week later guests gathered at the Liebelts' new Alice Spring home to celebrate not only Greg's milestone but the first birthday of his little brother, Clinton. Steve and Adele decided that because the boys' birthdays were only two weeks apart they would hold a joint party the weekend in between. It could start in the afternoon with a kids' show and drift into the evening with a barbecue and a few drinks for the adults—a sort of housewarming to mark their move back to town and a new phase of their lives. It would become the household standard, with separate birthday cakes and presents the only concession. The boys didn't mind the combined party; they adored each other. It seemed that in every photo taken of them Greg had his arm protectively around his little brother's shoulders. And everything that Greg did Clinton would follow in awe—even potty training.

The main topic of conversation that day was the dramatic release, 24 hours earlier, of Lindy Chamberlain. It seemed that the world's media had descended on the Territory overnight, to film her leaving

Darwin's Berrimah Jail. The discovery of Azaria's jacket, even without a body, was enough to overturn the emotion-charged murder conviction made four years before. As they relaxed in the evening cool, drinking beer and coaxing steaks on the well-used barbecue, opinions were as divided as in the rest of the country. Many were horrified that she had been released. No matter what the fresh evidence, there were those who would always believe that Lindy, pregnant again and emotionless at her trial, was guilty of cutting the infant's throat with a pair of nail scissors in the front seat of their yellow Torana and squashing the body into a camera bag until she had opportunity to dispose of it. They refused to believe that a dingo would sneak into a tent and grab a sleeping baby, instead remembering the sensational theory aired in the tabloids that the name Azaria meant 'sacrifice in the wilderness' and her death was a ritual desert killing somehow linked to their Seventh-Day Adventist background. The fact that Azaria actually meant 'gift from God' was somehow forgotten.

But others, less certain and probably a minority, insisted the murder made no sense and the discovery of the matinee jacket was proof that a dingo was responsible for the death. Lindy Chamberlain's defence team had always argued that the reason there was no dingo saliva on the baby's discarded jumpsuit was because she was wearing a matinee jacket over the top. The prosecution had dismissed the jacket as fiction. There was no saliva found, they had quipped, because sharp scissors don't salivate. Now the Chamberlains' claims had been vindicated. Perhaps the jury should have been more accepting of evidence given by the chief ranger, who had warned his superiors in Darwin a few weeks before the Chamberlain case that dingos at Ayers Rock had become so dangerous that 'children and babies can be considered possible prey'. Adele listened as the arguments went back and forth. She watched Greg drawing patterns in the dusty ground with a stick and Clinton falling on his backside for the umpteenth time as he took his first tentative steps, and hoped for the sake of all mothers that Lindy Chamberlain was an innocent and misunderstood woman.

* * *

Trevor Green fell in love with the idea of being a Northern Territory policeman long before he first set foot in Central Australia. The romance of the outback seemed to spring to life in the tales spun through the pages of books like Sydney Downer's *Patrol Indefinite* and Victor Hall's *Outback Policeman* that he read growing up in the Victorian goldfields around Ballarat. The years immediately after high school became a waiting game of a series of jobs and following the surf to northern Queensland until he turned 21 and qualified for entry into the khaki ranks.

His opportunity came in the wake of Cyclone Tracey which wrought her fury in the Christmas of 1974, flattening Darwin and creating havoc in communities across the Top End. Police officers were desperately needed and he was rushed through an eight-week training course in Adelaide before taking a train to Alice Springs and driving the rest of the way to Darwin.

Trevor threw himself into his new career, serving just 18 months on general duties before helping to establish an elite task force unit which specialised in the heavy end of police work—emergency response, search and rescue, anti-terrorism, surveillance and major crime. His next move was to the drug squad, where he was put in charge of the serious crime squad in Darwin. It was a meteoric rise that would not slow as he was moved to Tennant Creek as officer-in-charge and then to Alice Springs where he took charge of the CIB.

The first question Trevor would ask officers who came to him seeking a transfer from general duties to the CIB was how many arrests they had made over the previous six months and which were the most significant. With their records already in front of him he enjoyed watching the bullshit artists try to squirm their way out of the truth that they were talkers and not doers—and there was nothing Trevor Green hated more than someone who bragged about a non-existent arrest record.

Steve Liebelt was not a braggart and neither, in Trevor's mind, was he a man of straw. He had already been recommended to fill a vacancy in the overworked CIB ranks when he came to see Trevor a few months after returning from Kulgera. Steve wanted a new challenge away from general duties and saw the CIB as the way forward. Trevor Green agreed. The only question was whether he had the nous to be an investigator.

Trevor's team of 20 detectives could hardly keep up with the crime rate. Their beat extended south as far as the South Australian border and almost 1000 kilometres north, but it was in the town of 26 000 people where their biggest problems lay. Rarely a day went by in Alice Springs where there wasn't a bashing or rape victim waiting to be interviewed in the hospital's intensive care wing, caused mostly by violence within the indigenous community. But there were other factors which made the second biggest town in the Territory a crime hotspot, including its growing popularity as a tourist destination—which provided a steady stream of targets for robbery whose transience made it difficult to investigate cases. There was also a constant influx of criminals from the coastal cities who believed that Central Australia was a great place to hide but who typically left a trail of new crimes in their wake.

Steve Liebelt thrived in the hothouse environment of the CIB, quickly proving himself someone who could not only investigate a crime and make an arrest but also follow it through the system of paperwork and courtroom presentation to a successful prosecution. But there was a price to pay for the long hours and mateship that went hand in hand with the gruelling work—family life.

The new, government-provided home in Plumbago Crescent was modest but pleasant enough—three bedrooms with a shed at the end of a scrubby back lawn which turned to mud in the autumn rains or when the kids emptied the plastic swimming pool. But it somehow lacked the feel of the sprawling Kulgera complex with its broad verandahs and ring of eucalypts. Adele soon realised that something special had been lost in the move. She was still in Central Australia but it felt as though she had been dropped into the middle of suburbia. There was a dull sense of pressure, as if someone had handcuffed her to the kitchen sink. It was probably because Steve's working life had changed so suddenly and dramatically.

It soon became obvious that Steve was going to spend far less time at home here than at Kulgera. The workload was much bigger, not to mention the endless weeks of shiftwork which, inevitably, put a strain on home life with a young family. The types of crime Steve was dealing with had also become more serious; robberies, stabbings and rapes had replaced the rounds of cattle stations, traffic details and roadhouse punch-ups which were the bread and butter issues at Kulgera.

Their first Christmas in town epitomised the problem. They'd decided to give the boys bikes as their main presents. Greg, a few weeks from his fourth birthday, was getting a BMX bike. Clinton, almost two, was getting Greg's old bike, repainted of course, with new training wheels. Late on Christmas Eve, as they sat in the lounge room assembling and wrapping the bikes, the phone rang. A young girl had been raped at Ayers Rock and Steve was on call. She finished wrapping the bikes herself. The boys loved them but Steve wasn't there to join the fun; he didn't return until almost midnight on Boxing Day—gone for 48 hours. He would always recall the job; there was nothing festive about eating Christmas dinner alone in the restaurant at the Yulara resort while dealing with the trauma of a young girl kidnapped and raped by her own uncle.

The hardest thing for Adele, apart from having to attend social functions by herself, was dealing with the kids. At times she felt like a single mother. If Steve wasn't at work he was studying in the back room for his next police exam. It was the lot of a police officer—she knew that—but even knowing there were hundreds of other women and families in the same position didn't ease the frustration. It just made her wish for the ease of Kulgera when Steve was home for dinner most nights and they lived like a couple.

Adele took a part-time job at Kmart, working between 10 a.m. and 2 p.m. on weekdays handling lay-bys and bush orders to remote communities like Kulgera. The pay was useful but only confirmed the split in the family unit. Working at the pub in Kulgera had been like working next door, and weather readings had been done inside the police complex itself. Anyway, she didn't have kids then. It seemed as though she and Steve only crossed paths at the front door as she went to work and he got back home from a night shift.

The only blessing was that Debbie and Bronte Bruce had also moved from Kulgera, settling at Orange Creek station 100 kilometres west of Alice Springs. The experience of Kulgera was repeated as the two women repeatedly made the trip to the other's house. The following year, when Greg and Amanda were about to start preschool, Debbie and

Bronte moved permanently to Alice Springs. By this stage Adele was working for a car hire firm based at the airport so Debbie agreed to look after Greg and Clinton as well as her own children. Adele, who hated being alone in the house, was becoming increasingly agitated by Steve's workload and Bronte, who had taken work driving trucks, was also frequently on the road, so the two friends virtually lived in each other's homes. The children thought it was great, a very natural thing in their lives.

In the midst of the household of juggled hours and children, Steve's cousin Julie-Ann moved in. She was a troubled 12-year-old, clashing with her mother and constantly running away from home. What began as a period of welcome respite for both Julie-Ann and her mother became a permanent arrangement. In many ways her enlarged family provided Adele with some balance. Julie-Ann was old enough to do some babysitting, which allowed Adele and Steve to resume some social life. At the same time, Adele seemed to be a quieting influence on her niece. She understood that time of life as a young woman when nothing seemed to fit and everywhere was the wrong place. It took her back to her own teenage years, when the move from Toowoomba to Ocean Grove had dismantled her world.

Occasionally there would be reminders of the amazing but isolated world in which they lived. The working conditions of a Territory police officer provided airfares to officers and their families every two years to travel to any Australian capital city. It was in recognition of just how far many of them lived from families and the difficulty in travelling. Adele and Steve usually went to see their parents, either in Adelaide or the Gold Coast but one year, when Steve was in Darwin on a week's course, she took the children to visit her sister Katrina who still lived in Ocean Grove. It was a moment of nostalgia for Adele. She'd left behind the warmth of an Alice Springs winter for the bitter, windy cold of Southern Victoria in July. Greg had been to the beach once before, when they had stayed with her parents at the time of Clinton's birth, but Clinton had no notion of the sea. As they stood freezing on the sand hills above Collendia Beach Adele pointed over the choppy grey seas and said: 'Look Clinton, that's the sea.'

Clinton looked perplexed as he squinted into the distance: 'Where, Mummy? What's the sea?'

Adele had presumed that her three-year-old son knew what a beach and the sea looked like, maybe from books or television, but suddenly she realised that he had no concept of the ocean. He was a true son of the interior.

10
The desert has no logic

When he had given up all hope of survival, Simon Amos propped himself under a stunted tree, positioned the barrel of a .22-calibre rifle between his eyes and pulled the trigger. The 17-year-old could barely muster the strength, let alone the courage, but he could not bear the alternative, slower and far more painful death. The bullet was cold, clean and merciful.

The only person to hear the sharp report as it rippled and then faded to a memory in the shimmering heat haze was his mate, 16-year-old James Annetts, who still held out a faint hope for life as he staggered off along a narrow sandy track believing it would lead to rescue. Instead its path confirmed his own inevitable death. What the young jackaroo thought was a track was, in fact, a seismic survey line, carved precisely through the barren desert plains as part of a geometric reference grid used by mineral surveyors. They were the only humans apart from nomadic Aborigines to pass through this hell on earth called the Gibson Desert near the border of Western Australia and the Northern Territory. Amos and Annetts had walked an amazing 18 kilometres along this cul-de-sac of death, the rubber soles of their shoes disintegrating in the 55-degree surface heat in the December of 1986.

Months later, when the skeletal remains were finally discovered by a survey team, Annetts' dejected footprints would show that he had reached a T-junction before realising the fatal error. The boy turned back, retracing his path for several kilometres before he too gave up and prepared to die. There was no gun to end the pain swiftly, just an empty plastic water flask bought when he began his great adventure in the outback just four months before. In fun, he had scratched the words

'Take me back to Flora Valley' into its surface. His mind now caving in to dehydration and exhaustion to the point that it affected his spelling, the young man would scratch one last message—this time to comfort his parents and younger siblings: 'My follt. I allways love you mum and dad Jason Michelle and Joanne. I found peece.'

Annetts placed the flask on the track, pointing its bone-dry spout toward a small tree. His last physical act was to slump on the hot sand beneath its thin branches, not for its sparse shade but to wait. Psychiatrists would later surmise that the last minutes of this nightmare were probably calm; an incongruous serenity conjured from the acceptance of death as it approached and then claimed him.

The search for Simon Amos and James Annetts gripped the nation in a morbid fascination during that hottest of summers. There was anger that two naive teenagers, one from Adelaide and the other from a country town in New South Wales, had been allowed to answer advertisements a few months before to become jackaroos 'no experience necessary', to be left alone to manage two outstations of the remote cattle property of Flora Valley in the Kimberley region of Western Australia. It horrified even the toughest of outback communities where brawn was irrelevant without experience and common sense.

Their sudden and apparently reckless trek in an unreliable Datsun utility without four-wheel drive, and without enough food and water, perplexed police and the general public alike. Why had they suddenly left their posts? Were they homesick and fleeing from an adventure they were ill-prepared to face or merely probing further, unaware of their limitations in an environment that only the hardiest and canniest can survive? And where were they heading?

One theory, offered belatedly as the largely aerial search was abandoned a few weeks after their disappearance, was that they were trying to reach Alice Springs via a short cut offered to Amos by a truckie. Once in Alice, it would be a straight drive south along the Stuart Highway, past Kulgera, to Amos's home town of Adelaide. This theory appeared to be backed up by letters written by both teenagers to their families in the weeks before their disappearance, saying they would be coming home for a few days at Christmas before returning to the Kimberley.

Whatever the reason or destination, the pair had strayed from the roads they knew and where others travelled at least occasionally. They became lost 400 kilometres from home, and then hopelessly bogged on a narrow track which appeared to offer them a safe return to Flora Valley. All attempts to free the dilapidated vehicle from its sandy grave, including digging with its ripped-up sideboards, failed. Two batteries, including the spare, were flattened in their increasingly desperate attempts to start the ute. They decided, tragically, to walk, probably hoping to stumble on one of the two small Aboriginal communities they knew lay between them and Flora Valley station. Before they left the ute, the boys made an SOS sign on its bonnet. Other tools and bits of wood were laid out on the ground, pointing north where they would head.

But it was a signpost of ignorance, for they seemed to ignore basic survival techniques that might have saved them. They wore no hats and left behind matches that could have been used to light a fire and alert rescuers. Most tragically, they left a radiator full of water that was still drinkable four months later—in April 1987—when the seismic crews at last resumed their own, adventurous work.

There were signs of a makeshift campsite where, some days after they set out, the frightened boys shared their last meal, a tinned camp pie, and the last of their water supply before Amos made his decision. When his remains were found there was speculation of murder. There were also recriminations. Why had the ground and air search failed to cover the area where the skeletons were found? The parents of the boys spoke of confusion and a lack of coordination, even a refusal to call in other emergency services for help. Why had the search team not been bigger, with a wider range of opinions and options? Could they have been saved?

Senior police were defensive. There was no 'logical reason' for the youths to have been where their skeletons were found. The track was one of hundreds of grid tracks that criss-crossed inland Australia. There was no possibility that they could have turned off a major or a secondary road accidentally to get on the track. The track itself led nowhere. The search had been concentrated around known waterholes, to the northeast and west of Halls Creek, where it was considered more likely that the youths had been headed.

But the desert has no logic, only death for the unwary, careless or innocent.

*　*　*

The day that would irrevocably change the course of Steve Liebelt's life began innocently enough—a morning filled with tedious paperwork on a rape case he was covering and a decision to get out of the office to stretch his legs and buy lunch. The details escaped him when asked years later by former colleagues why he'd suddenly left the job, walking away from what most believed would be a stellar career. He wondered himself sometimes, not that he had any regrets.

As Steve walked down the mall someone shouted his name. He turned to see Damien Ryan standing by the entrance of his camera shop beckoning, with a smile across his face. He'd known Damien for years, firstly through the local football competition in the days before he and Adele went to Kulgera, later in his capacity as a cop covering a turf which included the roadhouse at Mount Ebenezer where Damien and his wife Jo held the lease.

Damien lived and breathed business. His father was one of Alice Spring's most successful entrepreneurs, a self-made millionaire, and Damien seemed intent on following in his footsteps. His enthusiasm was infectious and he and Steve would invariably end up talking about business opportunities when they got together. Nothing was ever concrete, just going into a partnership when the right opportunity came up. Steve loved the talk, for he harboured a quiet desire to strike out for himself. Damien always expected that Steve would make a move one day. It seemed to him that the force didn't offer quite enough for the big guy, even though he had established a reputation for himself as a bloody good copper, able to administer bush justice like few others.

Today Damien was obviously pleased with himself: 'Mate, I've got a real business proposition for you.'

Steve was non-committal: 'Ah yeah. What is it this time?'

'The lease has come up for the roadhouse at Dunmarra. The place is a bit run down, so they say, but why don't we have a look. I think Dave would be keen so we could split it three ways.'

Dave Sutcliffe was Damien's accountant. If it made sense to a bean counter then it was probably worth a look. 'Okay. Get some more details and let's have a look.'

As he walked away Steve felt a touch of excitement. He hadn't committed himself to anything but he'd just made the unconscious decision that if the proposition made sense financially he would make the leap. In the end, Steve Liebelt considered himself to be a doer; someone who didn't just talk about things but got out and did them. The idea of a business was an itch he simply had to scratch.

There was no reason to leave the force. If anything, Steve's career had shifted up a gear in recent months. He'd just passed his senior sergeant's exam and with almost two years under his belt at CIB there was the promise of steady promotion and the financial security of the public service. Then there was the camaraderie of the force. It was a brotherhood; a bond which meant that his wife and kids were safe when he had to go away overnight on a sudden job or to Darwin for a conference. It was part of the unwritten lore of the force that someone would go around to your house and make sure things were okay. He'd done it himself many times.

The thing that got Steve down at times was the debilitating impact of the crimes he faced every day—the mindless violence, the rapes, the child molestations, the devastation wrought by alcohol and drugs on families. It was especially hard when he knew the family of the victim, which in a town the size of Alice Springs was bound to happen from time to time. The paperwork he was doing before he saw Damien was one of those cases; the rape and bashing of a young woman whose father he knew well. The attacker had jemmied open a window of her unit in the middle of the night and used a curtain rod to stab and then bash her before sexually assaulting his semi-conscious victim. The injuries were horrific and it would take her months to recover from them. Steve could also see the psychological scars and knew they were permanent. When the attacker got off a few months later on a technicality Steve was furious. It insulted his sense that being a cop meant making a difference.

Steve knew Dunmarra. He'd been past dozens of times over the years. Roughly halfway along the 600-kilometre haul between

Katherine and Tennant Creek, it was famous for the characters who'd run the place—part of the rich folklore of outback life. The place was a bit run down mainly because it couldn't attract a lessee for more than a couple of years at a time and the owner, Shell, was reluctant to pour much money into a maintenance and renovation regime. This meant that regular travellers—the backbone of the roadhouse business—tended to bypass Dunmarra, timing their journeys to stop at a place that offered more. Damien reckoned the negatives were a positive because it meant the nine-year lease could be picked up for a good price.

The more Steve thought about it the better he liked the idea. Adele was unhappy about his not being home for her and the kids and letting the job take precedence, but that was the only way to get ahead. He was proud of what he had achieved; studied at every opportunity to complete his bank of examinations, attended every course that was going. Maybe it wasn't enough for the Liebelts as a family; maybe this business idea was the solution. They had all loved it at Kulgera, out in the bush, and this way they'd be working from home.

In February 1988, a few days after Clinton's third birthday, Steve and Damien drove to Dunmarra to have a closer look. A week later he was being counselled by a raft of senior officers, including Trevor Green, who'd been stunned when one of their most promising young officers had suddenly resigned. You should think it over, they told him; you're throwing away a bloody good career. You'll regret it later. Steve half agreed with them. He was jumping in without really knowing if he was in over his depth. There would be no looking back.

11
Dunmarra

Val Brooks was daydreaming behind the counter at the Golly It's Good café. She watched absently the handful of tourists drifting from one Aboriginal art gallery and souvenir shop to the next as they made their way up and down the Todd Street Mall. The mid-morning rush was over, and there would only be a handful of customers until lunch. The tables had all been reset and she'd even cleaned the coffee machine. There was nothing else to do but wait.

Val turned her attention to a young couple seated on a bench in animated discussion over what was obviously a map. Their accents and volume immediately identified them as American, their raggedy t-shirts and bandanas as backpackers. The town was filling with them, packed into the dozen or so hostels around town. March was a transition month in Alice Springs when the annual migration of employment fodder began. The young travellers who would staff the shops, bars, restaurants, hotels and motels over the winter tourist season were arriving ahead of the big-spending holidaymakers. It gave them a chance to settle into the rhythm of the place, or play the tourist thing themselves for a few weeks before the main game started. The mall would be awash with people within a month.

It made Val even more despondent about her own situation. It was not that she minded the work at the café. The hours and the customers were friendly enough and she got on well with the owner, Libby, but the pay was basic and, coupled with the cost of living in Alice Springs, this meant she was just managing to live from one pay day to the next. After rent, food and a bit of entertainment there was nothing much left out of her $250 a week. Val was 25 and had been in Alice Springs for three years. It was time to move on, probably back out bush to a roadhouse where it would be easier to save. She was no stranger to such places; had spent most of her working life in them in fact, ever since she left her home town of Angaston in the Barossa Valley at the age of 17. The last time, four years before, had been an eight-month stint as a cook at the Dunmarra roadhouse. She loved the sense of freedom found in small desert communities that outsiders saw as isolation.

Val's thoughts were interrupted by the arrival of her workmate, Mary Liebelt, to help prepare for the lunch crowd. The pair had discussed her predicament and vague plans a week or so before. You tend to learn a lot about the private lives of workmates behind a shop counter as the workload ebbs and flows through the day. Mary was old enough to be her mother but she was good to talk to; sympathetic even if she was unable to understand the desire to move to a smaller place. Alice Springs was small enough for someone who'd moved here from Adelaide.

Mary was eager to talk: 'What was the roadhouse you said you worked at a few years ago?' she asked with a half smile on her face.

'Dunmarra. It's up toward Darwin. Why?'

'You're not going to believe this, but Steve and Adele are going to buy the place. Steve's quitting the force and they're going to move the family up there.'

Val could sense an opportunity: 'Do they need any staff. Someone who could help them settle in?'

'I was hoping you'd say that. I mentioned you to them and they've got a proposition. But it's not what you think. They want you to be the governess for my two grandchildren.'

Val was a bit taken aback by the sudden turn of events and especially by the offer to work as a governess. She'd never done anything like it before though she knew a number of girls who'd worked out on stations taking care of the owners' children. But she liked kids and it had to be more interesting than standing behind a shop counter all day.

It was settled over a cup of coffee at the Liebelt house a few days later. Steve and Adele were friendly and laid back, happy to accept Mary's recommendation even though Val had no experience as a governess. Adele knew what she wanted. In her view, the job didn't need qualifications, just a love of children and a fair whack of common sense.

Val Brooks qualified on both counts. There was also something familiar in her life story, not unlike that of Debbie Bruce, Candy Kerr or even her own experiences—all young women who'd ventured into Central Australia to see what life was about, liked what they saw and stayed.

Val had grown up in and around the small villages of the Barossa Valley. Like Adele, she had left school early to work in a local shop and moved out of home soon after discovering financial independence, but in Val's case there was something more important to be tested. She and her sister Karen were identical twins—numbers three and four in a family of six sisters—and by the age of 17 both had grown tired of being constantly referred to as a pair. The only way to be seen as individuals, of being called by their names instead of being 'the twins this and the twins that', was to go their separate ways. Karen headed to the coast, settling on Kangaroo Island off Adelaide. Val went in the opposite direction, inland to the tiny township of Kingoonya—a one pub, garage and general store settlement which at the turn of the century had been a tiny but bustling gold mining town. By the time Val Brooks arrived in 1980 it had been reduced to a flyspeck, halfway between Port Augusta and Coober Pedy. Later, when the Stuart Highway was sealed, bypassing Kingoonya, the township all but disappeared.

Val had worked in the hotel, one of two women whose shifts could include serving at the bar or cleaning rooms, depending on the number of guests. She loved it because for the first time in her life she was an individual. It was here that Val met her best friend, Kathy. Somehow the friendships made in an environment like Kingoonya seemed deeper than the myriad friendships she'd had at school; probably because there wasn't anyone else and you had to make sure the friendship lasted. The work petered out in early 1981 and Val moved further north, aiming to reach Darwin so she could say that she'd crossed the continent from south to north. Ayers Rock was the next stop. She arrived in the months after the Azaria Chamberlain incident and watched the impact of the controversy as she worked in the kitchen of the Ayers Rock Chalet. Alice Springs followed, then Dunmarra, then Darwin. But the coast was not for her and she headed inland back to Alice Springs, where she'd been ever since.

Greg and Clinton took to Val immediately and she obviously liked them. Both looked like their mother, with their white-blond hair and blue eyes, but were clearly going to be as big as their father. Five-year-old Greg was cheeky in a nice sort of way, handling the job interview himself as he peppered her with questions about what she would and wouldn't let them do or eat. Clinton, just past his third birthday, was more reserved, happy to let his big brother make the running as he listened to her promises of fun and adventure and a schoolroom with a computer and a radio. The last thing to be negotiated was her name. 'Miss Brooks' was far too formal considering the amount of time they would spend together each day, and 'Val' was a little too casual considering the professional relationship she had to develop. There had to be some level of authority. They compromised—'Miss Val', it would be.

* * *

It took just two days at Dunmarra for the first snake scare. A deadly two-metre king brown appeared at the front door around 10 p.m. as they were still trying to unpack and get things ready for a trip to Katherine the next morning to enrol the boys at the School of the Air. Adele knew immediately that the olive brown reptile was not only big but venomous and slammed the door as it slithered across the path toward the light. She, Val, Julie-Ann and the kids were trapped. Steve had gone back to Alice Springs and there was no intercom linking the main house to the roadhouse where one of the men could be called on to get rid of the snake with a gun or shovel. After a half-hour stand-off, Julie-Ann decided to go for help. She opened the door, leapt over the front step and ran.

The snake, oblivious to the panic, had undoubtedly slipped under the house; a nocturnal predator probably looking for a frog or a mouse which were both in abundance around the house and sheds. Dealing with mouse plague at Kulgera had been one thing, but a potentially deadly snake about the house was entirely another. Adele woke the boys, who had settled remarkably well into their new bedroom, and the three of them also sprinted over to the roadhouse. Their decision to stay out of the way was fortuitous. Minutes later they heard the sharp crack of a .22, followed by the rattle of shattered glass. The rifle had gone off accidentally as one of the men stood up after flashing his torch under the house. The bullet went through the wall of the toilet, narrowly missing the bowl, through the open door into the combined kitchen and lounge area before smashing through a window and embedding itself in a tree outside. The snake was never found.

The incident was the last straw in 48 hours of mayhem since their arrival. The furniture had been driven up the week before and stored at the back of the carport. By the time they arrived, their belongings were crawling with huge bloody cockroaches. It seemed there were thousands of them as Adele dropped a boxful of pots and pans, unleashing an eruption of the black scuttling plague. It would take months to get rid of them. Even paying the kids 10 cents for every cockroach they could stomp to death barely made a dent in their numbers. Finally, the pest control company agreed to drive out from Katherine and spray the place—but it would take several trips to wipe them out. What a start to the world of private enterprise!

Events had moved quickly. It seemed just a few weeks since Steve raised the possibility of chucking in his job and buying a roadhouse. It came as a complete surprise to Adele, though she knew he'd always harboured a desire to run his own business. While living at Kulgera they'd occasionally driven to Mount Ebenezer for a couple of days to see Damien Ryan and his then girlfriend, Joanne. Other than football, Damien and Steve had always seemed to talk about business when they got together. It was inevitable, she supposed, that he would give in to the desire one day. Adele raised no objection other than demanding an acknowledgment from Steve that they were taking a risk moving from the protective umbrella of government employment to the unstable world of private enterprise. He agreed. They'd both watched Peter and Maria Bohem struggle to make a living at Kulgera, relying on the regular trade of locals and passing truckies when the tourist buses slowed during the blazing summer months. There were no guarantees that they'd make a fist of things at Dunmarra.

Adele and Steve had driven out of Alice Springs with the boys on April Fool's Day but it was a harrowing exit. The rain had started to fall the night before—a deluge geologists would later claim had not been seen in over 500 years and certainly not since European settlement. By morning more than 300 millimetres had fallen and the normally dry Todd River had burst its banks and was flooding the town. As Adele and the boys watched from the safety of the northern bank, they realised that an Aboriginal man and his wife had become trapped in the middle of the raging torrent, clinging to what was normally a safe riverbed campsite on a small hillock that had now become an island. As the crowd built up, it became obvious the couple would have to be rescued or they would drown. Neither seemed to be able to hear above the roar of the water the crowd's instructions that they climb a tree until the police helicopter could be called. Both were confused and frightened of the rising water. Like most of the town's black population, they could not swim. Finally help arrived. The man was plucked to safety but instead of waiting, and to the shock of the audience of several hundred, the woman hurled herself into the waters and was swept away. Her body was found a few hours later. Two others died that day in similar circumstances.

Later that day, just outside the town of Tennant Creek which lies 500 kilometres north of Alice Springs, Steve and Adele caught up with Trevor Green who had left town the day before on his way to Darwin in a career transfer that would take him on to become the Territory's youngest ever assistant commissioner. They drove the next 300 kilometres in convoy before parting company and careers, but not friendship, as the Liebelts pulled into the driveway at Dunmarra.

Adele felt a sense of relief and even excitement about the prospect of something different. She had never really settled back into the Alice Springs lifestyle despite all the advantages of a big town. She had been far more comfortable in a place the size of Kulgera, and Dunmarra was even smaller. The house was small but functional enough, an unremarkable fibro transportable set on stumps and dating back to the seventies when Dunmarra was rebuilt after being burned down. Time and the semi-tropical heat had given it a respectable lawn and a flourishing bougainvillea which covered the end wall in vibrant purple. It had all the modern conveniences—power, telephone, running water and air-conditioning—which had become a mandatory feature of living in the outback.

The business itself was a sprawling complex consisting of a caravan park, motel, petrol station, bar and takeaway food section/restaurant. They had 14 staff though, as inevitably happens with a management change, many would be replaced within the first few months. There were eight motel rooms, each with a couple of single beds and a bathroom; 10 powered sites in the caravan park, and a huge area for the campers who would be their main clientele. Out the back of the roadhouse there was a generator/storeroom, a jumble of sheds in various states of dilapidation and a line of staff rooms providing accommodation only marginally better than the motel suites. The front of the roadhouse was dominated by a massive bulldozed apron so the road trains could slide off the highway and park without having to manoeuvre.

The first and most obvious need was to plant some trees. Though surrounded by dense and inhospitable bullwaddy scrub, the complex itself was treeless barring one mahogany out the front which, they were told by a local white man—a government advisor for the Aboriginal camp at nearby Elliott—had a place in local dreaming mythology: the tree was a woman punished because she had fallen in love with a man from a rival tribe. Angry elders transformed her into a wildcat—the tree—and so she stood, guarding the entrance to a white man's roadhouse. Adele always doubted the tale. It had a touch of Romeo and Juliet about it and she didn't trust government advisors. One day they stumbled across a photograph of Dunmarra taken in the 1940s: there was no tree. True or not, the women of the Elliott tribe did consider Dunmarra a place of mystery—'bad spirit country' they would remark without further explanation. Whenever they arrived to buy supplies the women would swish branches out the front before coming inside, as if to sweep away the evil they feared.

12
Chooks in the bedrooms

Of all the men and women who would follow in his determined footsteps, few embodied the frontier spirit of Australia's desolate north better than the nineteenth-century surveyor-turned-explorer John MacDouall Stuart. Between 1848 and 1863 this diminutive Scotsman mounted half a dozen fearless expeditions into the uncharted and mysterious interior of the new land. On each occasion he pushed further than anyone had before, accurately mapping grazing land and cattle runs as well as possible mining sites for copper and gold. For months at a time he would live in the wilderness, battling the ravages of scurvy and losing an eye in his quest to pave the way for settlement.

Three times he ventured into the forbidding stony plains north of Adelaide with a small band of men and a few dozen horses to attempt the impossible and cross the continent from bottom to top through its fiery heart. But each time he was driven back, firstly by the Macdonnell Ranges guarding what would later become the city of Alice Springs and then, further north, by a desert forest he could neither penetrate nor skirt. A diary note voiced his frustration at being baulked by the thick, tangled scrub: 'We have not seen a bird or the chirp of any to disturb the gloomy silence of the dark and dismal forest.' That place was the land around Dunmarra.

Stuart's eventual success at his third attempt in 1862 marked the path for the overland telegraph line, which linked the Australian colonies with the rest of the world two decades after his triumphant return to the cheering crowds of Adelaide, ironically on the same day that Melbourne mourned the loss of explorers Burke and Wills.

Stuart's deeds ranked him not only as Australia's most successful inland explorer but also one whose understanding of the land he traversed meant his expeditions never cost a single life. What others saw as an alien and terrifying landscape was to Stuart—a restless misfit who hated sleeping indoors—an awe-inspiring work of nature and a place of personal freedom. Stuart made no fortune from his explorations, won little formal adulation in his lifetime and died in virtual obscurity back in England.

He repaid those who privately funded his journeys by naming pieces of Central Australia after members of their families. The Finke River bears the name of his friend William Finke and the town of Tennant Creek was named after another friend, John Tennant. By far his biggest benefactor was the South Australian pastoralist James Chambers, who ran cattle on much of the land Stuart surveyed in three earlier expeditions. Thus the creeks and rivers, mountains and gorges which trace his route north bear incongruous names such as Priscilla, Fanny, Anna, Mary, Charles, James and John. So too does the Territory's third biggest town—Katherine—which Stuart named after James Chambers's second daughter.

One of Stuart's team members, Benjamin Head, would later recall his leader's prowess in the bush: 'You could not beat the little fellow, no matter who it might be. He had the instincts of a bushman. However foolish he may have been in town, there is not a man in Australia can say a word against him as a leader in the bush. I never came across the like of him.'

Within seven years of Stuart's triumph the South Australian Government agreed to build a 3200-kilometre overland telegraph line connecting Adelaide to Darwin if the British-Australian Telegraph Company would lay a submarine cable from Java to Darwin, enabling Australia to speak with the rest of the world. It was one of the greatest engineering achievements of the century, completed in less than two years after hauling 36 000 timber poles, insulators and unnumbered tonnes of wire through the merciless country from either end of the line. Afghan camels were used to transport supplies and 2000 sheep were taken to ensure fresh meat. The route followed largely in Stuart's footsteps with exploring parties scouting ahead of the construction teams to find waterholes. One of the surveyors remarked: 'Anyone travelling to the Northern Territory, having Stuart's diary with the country described so accurately, could not possibly make a mistake. I consider he was the king of our explorers.'

It was 27 kilometres south of Dunmarra that the construction team moving up from the south met the team which had been building the line from the north. A monument was later built beside the Stuart Highway to commemorate the accomplishment. The plaque read in part:

> The Overland Telegraph Line. This plaque was erected in memory of Sir Charles Todd, Postmaster-General of the Province of South Australia. His gallant construction teams, operators, and linesmen...the northern and southern parts of this epic overland telegraph line were finally joined about one mile west of this spot by R. C. Paterson, engineer, at 3.15 p.m. on Thursday August 22, 1872 thus making possible for the first time instantaneous telegraph communication between Australia and Great Britain.

Six men perished building the line. One of them was named Dan O'Mara—an Irishman, or so his heritage was assumed, who died a lonely and horrific death after he wandered off into the unforgiving desert forest noted years before by Stuart. A massive search was launched but his body was never found. Nothing else was recorded about the man, what he looked like, if he had a family or why he came to Central Australia. Even the Aboriginal trackers brought in to help find the unfortunate fellow mispronounced his name. They called him Dunmarra.

* * *

Ken and Margaret Blanchard stopped at Dunmarra at least six times between 1947 and 1957. It is likely they spent at least a few nights there over the years but that is not why they are remembered. The West Australian couple recorded their passing by scratching their names and the dates of their visits, even the cars they drove, into the side of an old steel tank which sits hidden among the trees behind the old

No. 6 bore on the other side of the highway from the roadhouse. The first time they stopped was on 7 February 1947, long before the highway was sealed, when they drove a 1934 Chevy Tourer. They were mostly driving Holdens when they returned late in the same year, then in 1948, 1949, 1953 and finally on 7 August 1957.

The Blanchards weren't the first to use the tank to mark their passing. Soldiers on their way north during World War II also found it. Most of the etchings had faded over the years but one could imagine the camaraderie of young men like 'Blue' Hutchison and his mates Corporal S.M. Haart, R.G. Wilson and F.W. Walker who stopped for a drink and a patch of shade on New Year's Day in 1944. Like the early explorers of the last century, they wanted to leave their mark on a land that dared to be traversed.

The walls inside the roadhouse told a graphic story; covered in framed, grainy black-and-white photographs which followed the tiny settlement's history and its passing parade of human drama and ingenuity. There were the early road trains of Kurt Johannsen, the Alice Springs-born inventor and mailman who revolutionised transport when he developed a system which allowed a prime mover to pull several trailers at once, and who once used petrol drums to float his truck across flooded rivers and get the mail and supplies through to cattle stations in the district.

Above all, however, the photos celebrated the human spirit of the outback. Two faces in particular peered out at patrons from shots of yesteryear, when the bar was dominated by a fan to keep customers cool under the corrugated iron roof and the highway outside was little more than a dirt track which limited a day's travel to something less than 100 kilometres. The story of Noel and 'Ma' Healey began in January 1951 when a young woman named Thelma Greening stepped off the bus at Dunmarra when it stopped overnight on its way to Darwin. Just why Miss Greening was going north was never known but when the bus left the next morning she wasn't aboard. The roadhouse owner, Noel Healey, had apparently taken an overnight fancy to Thelma and, according to later tales, shanghaied the former Melbourne convent nurse. The fact that Thelma and Noel married later that year tended to discount the colourful theory that she had been an unwilling participant. Either way, the union created one of the Territory's most enduring and eccentric couples.

When Darwin historian Peter Forrest compiled an unpublished paper on Dunmarra in 1999, there was no shortage of tales about big, brawling Noel and tiny, gregarious Ma, as she became known. They epitomised the character and acerbic generosity of the outback, playing host through two decades as air-conditioning and running water turned the roadhouse from a virtual bush camp into a welcome though ramshackle stopping point on the long haul north.

Noel was already a Territory legend when Ma came along; a pioneer in the truest sense of the word. English born, he'd come to Australia in 1910 and reached the Territory in 1923 via Queensland where he operated a trucking firm in the state's north-west. Noel settled in Katherine with his then wife, Gem, and three children, and began a new business carting supplies to distant stations and townships. Over the next decade he carted salt from the Gulf and machinery for the bores along the Barkly stock route, and cut posts for the Canning stock route into Western Australia. He even helped install naval guns at East Point in Darwin.

Noel branched out in 1934, buying Dunmarra station, which had been established a few years before by pioneers John and Katherine McCarthy. He ran a small and somewhat dubious livestock business, which he supported by cutting and selling bush timber for use in the mine shafts of Timber Creek as well as selling refreshments to travellers on the dirt track which was later to become the Stuart Highway.

By 1941 Noel had rebuilt the Dunmarra homestead and was granted a liquor licence which he operated from a roadside bar carved out of the local bush timber. It won both praise and criticism. A 1943 magazine article critiqued roadside inns across the Territory:

> …Lancewoods and dark bullwaddy trees lead you gradually to the forest country. Just on the edge of this is Dunmarra station. We used to call there in the early days for a glass of fresh cow's milk brought by a good old black gin from a canvas cooler safe under creepers on the back verandah. Cows are kept here, and you can see them making to the dam among tall gums at evening, and there always seemed horses snorting in the nearby yard.

You still can have your glass of milk, and still see the cows and hear the horses, but a little closer to the road is a second house, and beer and cold drinks are all day long served out to soldiers. This bar is rather a wonderful place for it is beautifully built of the local timbers and the black ebony—bullwaddy and lancewood—shows in the front of the counter. Stockmen now mind the run, the owner stands behind the bar and a tall, good looking wife directs the gins. They have given over four thousand meals to men in the Services—it being their pleasure and generosity to do so. Long in the minds of travellers during these days of war will the hospitality of the host and hostess of Dunmarra be a pleasant memory to recall.

Others were not so generous, accusing the Healys of ripping off the Australian troops with overpriced booze as they travelled north to Darwin. One army historian noted:

Sixty miles north of Elliott was Dunmarra station then owned by Noel Healey. In April 1942 Mr Healey erected a log booth at the roadside and secured a liquor licence. [There was] no bargain with soft drink selling at one shilling and sixpence, a bottle of beer six shillings and the drink, no matter what the label, often tasted more like the drainings from wet straw than the satisfying drink intended by the manufacturer.

A police historian also accused Gem Healy of selling liquor at exorbitant prices: 'whiskey at five pounds per bottle, beer at five shillings per bottle and cider at six shillings per bottle'.

Noel and Gem Healey divorced in 1948. Then Ma arrived and took Gem's place. Over the next 20 years Dunmarra developed a reputation as a ramshackle but friendly stopover where the food was inedible and the accommodation Spartan—but the beer was cold and the parties legendary.

Life at Dunmarra was unpredictable, but the hospitality was always assured. Truck driver John Maddock dropped in one day with a mate. They both ordered a steak. 'Ma Healey went out the back and there was a helluva commotion. After a while she came back with two cooked steaks and muttering about the bloody cat which she'd found nibbling at one of the pieces. I still don't know which one of us got the nibbled bit. After that I always ordered tinned stuff.'

Ian Cawood was another truckie who would recall the strange cooking habits of Ma Healey: 'I was yarning with another driver outside the Healeys' place at Dunmarra one day and we decided to see if Ma would knock up something for us. Noel and Ma had been away for a while and had only just arrived back. The place was a bit of a shambles, but they knew they would find something around the place that would go towards meeting our needs. At Dunmarra you could always expect the unexpected. Occasionally there would be a pet pig in the bar, there always seemed to be a few chooks walking in and out of the front door and flying onto the bar counter. And if you happened to go out into the dining room for a meal there would always be a dog or two sprawled out under the tables. Well, we asked if we could get something to eat and Ma said she could make a couple of hamburgers. We thought that sounded pretty good so we had a couple of beers while we waited. In came the hamburgers eventually and we sat down to devour them but we soon realised we weren't going to be able to eat them. From the first mouthful it became evident that she didn't have any lettuce or cabbage so she had done her best to oblige and garnished them with grass. We just couldn't cope with those hamburgers. We offered them to the dogs and they just turned up their noses at them.'

In the 1960s when the Buchanan Highway was being bulldozed through the scrub, Rowena Stroud stayed at Dunmarra with her three children: 'I had three kids and Ma was very good to us. When the tank ran over she would say, "The tank's running over, now's the time to have a bath', and we would all strip off and get under the overflow and have a wash. They had new air-conditioned motel rooms down there then and people would break their journeys during the day and sleep in one of the rooms. This was before air-conditioned cars and people would drive all night when it was cooler. But Dunmarra was still pretty rough. Ma used to serve porridge from a camp oven, but when there was no porridge in it the camp oven was home to new piglets about the place.'

For some reason Ma Healey could not stand public servants. On one occasion a man walked into the bar wearing a white shirt and long socks.

Ma picked him for a public servant. He asked for petrol. 'No chance,' Ma snorted. 'Been out of petrol for two days.' She turned and resumed her conversation at the bar. There was plenty of petrol for anyone else.

It would be an understatement to say the accommodation was basic. Steve Martin recalled stopping in at Dunmarra one night on the way back to Melbourne from Darwin. It was late at night and they banged on the door. Ma Healey came out: 'We asked if there was any accommodation and Mrs Healey took us to what seemed like a barn with bare earth floors, the space divided into rooms by hanging hessian. We were a bit disillusioned. We then asked if there was a shower. Mrs Healey told us to follow her and she went through one of the hessian dividers into what she said was the bridal suite. There was a couple asleep on an old army type wire stretcher. She took us out the back to a 44-gallon drum full of scummy water. We then drove out to Larrimah where we stayed the night.'

Terri Hinde and her husband Aubrey, a bookmaker, were frequent visitors during the 1960s. Terri told the story of how they stopped in once when she was sick: 'Ma made chicken broth for me. She killed the chicken especially and sat with me until I finished the broth. She nursed me and looked after me wonderfully. She wore grubby old shapeless cotton print dresses, calf length—she said she was too busy to sew up more of them. They had shirred elastic waists and the elastic had gone. I never saw her in shoes; always in thongs or bare feet. Her hair was pulled straight back, kept in place by an Alice band. She always had a pig following her like a dog. There were chooks everywhere, and they all had names.

'I sometimes saw her poking the copper with a clothes stick and I thought she was boiling clothes, but she was boiling corned beef. There was a big thick scum over the water. They served enormous sandwiches. She would cut just four slices of bread from a loaf then add slabs of beef and raw chopped onions. You wouldn't believe it, but people liked them. There was always someone in the bar and on Saturdays the place would be really jumping. Ma was always busy, but Noel would stand behind the bar and yarn. Ma would stand on a box high enough to cut the sandwiches. She would be at one end of the bar and Noel at the other, entertaining. Noel went out of his way to entertain the ladies, especially the young good-looking ones.'

Mac Clark called into Dunmarra in 1962 with an agent from Elders. They decided to stay the night and were given bedrooms. Mac went to sleep but the agent was disturbed by loud groaning noises from the next room. It went on for most of the night. Eventually he could contain his anxiety no longer so he got up and bashed on the door from where the noises were coming. There was no reply, just more groaning, so he pushed open the door. Inside he saw a sow and 10 newborn piglets. He rushed in and hunted the sow out of the room. She ran off through the opposite wall and took the wall with her.

Theo Kelley, writing in *The Territorian* in December 1965, described Dunmarra as:

> a dilapidated symphony of corrugated iron and bougainvillea with grey and pink galahs—a cozy makeshift oasis of petrol bowsers, fly deterrent, rainbow streamer doorways, plastic flowers, corrugated bed sheets, hot cold water, uncertain plumbing—and the inevitable steak and eggs—a place where you can meet up with pythons in the dining room, chooks in the bedrooms and an endless stream of fantastic characters in the bar.

Noel Healy died of pneumonia in 1970, though most believed his demise was due more to a bashing he'd received while trying to stop two men stealing a car battery. After his death Thelma went back to Victoria before returning to the Territory in 1990 and settling in Tennant Creek. In the ensuing two decades, the Dunmarra roadhouse had been demolished and rebuilt and gone through a series of lessees, the latest of whom were Steve and Adele Liebelt.

13
A teddy named Victor

Adele's view of life had turned a remarkable circle from that young woman who had sat in a Kombi van outside the Ti Tree police station in April 1979 wondering how anyone could live in such an isolated, dust-soaked outpost. Nine years later, now with a husband and two young children, Adele had made just such a decision as she had absently wondered about that day. The only difference was that Dunmarra was even smaller and more isolated than Ti Tree.

Adele soon learned that no rehearsals or allowances are made in the world of private enterprise, not even for motherhood. Though she was well versed in the routine of running a roadhouse, from the bowser to the kitchen, it had been as an employee on casual shifts, not as the owner taking all the financial risks. Her days would now begin at 5 a.m. seven days a week, opening the dining room to dole generous piles of steak and eggs onto the plates of hungry truckies, and end 12 hours later, after an afternoon spent in the cluttered office collating and processing the piles of paperwork that seemed to accumulate exponentially with the success of their venture. Steve looked after the fuel service and accommodation sites.

Their timing, as it turned out, was impeccable. This was 1988, Australia's bicentennial year, and the nationwide celebrations included a re-enactment of the great cattle drives of the last century. Within a fortnight of taking over the business more than 6000 people flocked to Newcastle Waters, 80 kilometres to the south, to witness the beginning of a 2000-kilometre drive to Longreach in Queensland. It was a three-day festival, including a colonial ball and culminating in the send-off of the droving party who would take two months to make their journey.

For the Liebelts it was a chaotic but welcome start to their new life as the roadhouse buzzed with activity from the passing traffic. Adele made over a thousand rounds of sandwiches that weekend and went through two weeks' supplies of pies and pasties.

Dunmarra would be on the national map again within months as one of the checkpoints for the first World Solar Challenge car race. The 3000-kilometre race from Darwin to Adelaide was the brainchild of Danish-born adventurer Hans Tholstrup who had met and become friends with Steve Liebelt in 1982 when he stopped at Kulgera on his way across Australia in a solar-powered car. The Solar Challenge attracted worldwide interest, not just because of the technology it helped develop but also because of the landscape through which the testing course was run.

The Liebelt children had also to be settled into their new environment, one in which there was no neighbourhood playmate closer than the nearest cattle station. The morning after the snake scare Adele and Miss Val had driven to Katherine, 300 kilometres north, to enrol the kids in school. Julie-Ann would board at the town's high school and bus home to Dunmarra at weekends and the boys would become students of the Territory's famous School of the Air. From its palm-fringed headquarters on the banks of the Katherine River the school boasted the world's largest classroom, with 200 pupils spread out across 800 000 square kilometres of the top end of Australia—an area twice the size of Texas and three times bigger than the United Kingdom.

Adele and Steve set up a schoolroom in an old staffroom at the back of the complex, where school began promptly at 8.30 a.m. and finished at 3 p.m., all under the tutelage of Miss Val. The boys' schoolwork would arrive by post and they would participate in two half-hour radio lessons each day. The schoolroom was to become a focal point of life at Dunmarra. Even the staff members became involved, listening to the boys read or helping them with art classes. The walls became the diary of their progress as they were painted and repainted to follow childhood fads and current affairs by anyone who could hold a brush. The year after the family arrived at Dunmarra the army held major exercises in the region—Kangaroo '89—so the boys painted the walls in army camouflage. The next year packs of dinosaurs roamed across the walls, while one of Greg's teachers spent a weekend painting the outside walls in scenes of Teenage Mutant Ninja Turtles and Batman.

The school and its teachers played a bigger role than just voices at the other end of a two-way radio. Staff visited regularly and many became family friends. Twice a year—in May and December—there was a school camp where the kids were placed with their teachers and peers in a normal classroom situation. The May camp ended with a sports carnival and the December camp included swimming classes. The Liebelt brothers excelled at both. Homecomings after a sporting carnival included finding more wall space to hang the clusters of ribbons Greg and Clinton inevitably brought with them.

Students were not only organised into ages but geographical clusters, each with its own teacher. The Buchanan cluster, which covered the settlements and stations along the Stuart Highway between Mataranka and Elliott, had its own get-together once a year as well, when the few dozen students would gather at one of the homes for a week of school and activities. Adele and Steve hosted several gatherings at the roadhouse, the sprawling camping site and motel units providing plenty of space to accommodate the students and their families. These were special times; a rare occasion when the children of a neighbourhood were able to get together and interact as a group instead of as a faceless gaggle of voices.

The get-togethers were just as important for parents as their children separated physically by hundreds of kilometres. Adele became heavily involved in the Isolated Children's Parents Association, secretary for the Katherine branch and a state councillor with the portfolio of boarding schools. Like their children, association members met over the radio, battling poor reception which more than a decade later meant that radio and mobile phone reception was still impossible for all but a few kilometres on the road from Katherine to Tennant Creek.

It was at a school function that Adele met Janelle Underwood who, with her husband Reg, ran the Bunda cattle station near the border with Western Australia. Between them lay 600 kilometres of desolate desert and scrub but the two women gelled as easily as Adele and Debbie Bruce did years before. This friendship, sustained by phone calls and the occasional family holiday, was as strong as if they lived next door with a picket fence between them. As they met and laughed over an accident involving a spilled cup of coffee, Adele's son Greg and Janelle's son Mitch were meeting in the playground. Theirs too would become a lifelong friendship.

The only thing that worried Adele about living in such isolation with two young children was the interaction that Greg and Clinton missed out on compared to children growing up in town. She contented herself with the notion that they were luckier than many other Territory children, like the Underwoods' three daughters and one son, who lived on remote stations where stockmen and horses were the only passing trade. At least living in a prominent roadhouse meant there was always people coming and going. Transport was accessible and a 600-kilometre round trip to Katherine on a Saturday for sport or a social activity was not uncommon.

* * *

The biggest and smallest men on an Australian Rules football team must develop a special on-field bond, if only because one needs the other to make their own performance complete. A ruckman wants a smart, nippy rover to anticipate where he is going to palm the ball at a bounce-down or boundary throw-in, and a rover will never get a touch of the ball unless his ruckman wins a fair share of the aerial contests. That about summed up the relationship between Steve Liebelt and Andy McLay when they met at the Rovers Football Club in 1976. Steve was the lanky 19-year-old ruckman, drafted to Alice Springs on the strength of a couple of reserves games he'd played in the South Australian league, and Andy was the little man at his feet—though he would privately grumble that his big mate tended to favour the team's ruck-rover, 'Bushy' Pickford, with his palming skills. Either way, their partnership was an important element in the club's triumphant premiership two years later. It was also the spark for a friendship that went far beyond a mere sporting collaboration.

Andy stayed in touch after their footballing days were over. He was a guest at Steve and Adele's wedding and, by chance, moved to Katherine with his job as an electrical fitter for the NT Department of

Transport and Works in the same year the Liebelts moved to Dunmarra. He would drop in and say hello on his way up and down the highway, and Steve would stop for a beer when he went to town for the day. He even responded to Andy's badgering and chucked in $500 to become a sponsor of a local football club—the Katherine Hawks—with which Andy had become involved. He didn't care that the money only entitled him to having the Dunmarra Wayside Inn logo printed on the back of a few dozen t-shirts worn by players who already knew the place. That wasn't the point. He was helping out a team which was needed to build a local competition, and towns like Katherine needed sporting teams. Andy put it another way: 'Some of the best friendships you ever make are around footy clubs. If you become associated with a footy club then you'll have mates for life, and they will always be there when you need them.'

Andy was one of those blokes that everybody liked. He loved to sit at the bar and strike up a conversation with anyone sitting nearby, particularly about his beloved St Kilda. God knows why a boy from Port Augusta in South Australia would barrack for a Melbourne team, but the fact that the Saints hadn't won a flag since 1966 only firmed his convictions. Nor would he change horses with the promised inclusion of an Adelaide team in the AFL competition. But behind the sunny, carefree mask lurked a sad story. Andy always suspected, or perhaps feared that he would one day be struck down with the degenerative disease muscular dystrophy. His mother had died from its ravages and the chances that he or his siblings carried the gene were high. It was a game of Russian roulette that made living with the expectation almost as bad as the reality. It was why he would never marry or have children, he once confided to Adele. Instead, the social circle he created became his family.

Andy's fears were confirmed in late 1989 when, at the age of 40, he was diagnosed with the disease. It began a game of cat and mouse in which he and his doctors could only guess how long it would take for his body to waste to a point where he couldn't drive a car, would be forced to rely on a walking stick or a wheelchair and, inevitably, lose his independence to full-time nursing care.

The first casualty of this war of attrition was Andy's working career. He stayed in the workshops for 18 months until he was forced onto sick leave while the department's medical staff considered whether he could be employed elsewhere or should be pensioned off. It was an awful time psychologically, watching others making decisions about his physical capability and, ultimately, his worth. Steve Liebelt stepped in and offered Andy a bed at Dunmarra—a place to stay while the rusted wheels of bureaucracy slowly ground away. Andy also had to make permanent living arrangements for an uncertain future. He moved in with his sister back in Port Augusta but the arrangement lasted only a few months. A broken hip forced him to use a cane and the change in climate exacerbated the pain he endured. His world was shattered completely when his sister was also diagnosed with the disease. He had to leave.

It took one phone call to Steve in July 1992 for Dunmarra to become Andy's permanent home. 'I can't stay in Port Augusta. Can I come back to Dunmarra?' was all he asked. Steve made the 1600-kilometre trip the next day to pick up his mate. By the time they returned, one of the motel units had been set up for him, and Andy McLay moved in for the next five years. He had a government pension but no money ever changed hands between him and Steve; there was an unspoken mates' agreement that he was now part of the roadhouse family. When the staff cleaned the motel units they also cleaned Andy's room and when they cooked meals for the restaurant they also cooked for Andy. In exchange he became the Dunmarra watchman, looking after the roadhouse generators and air-conditioning units and operating the fuel cash register. He warned Steve about accepting cheques from truckies for hundreds of dollars in fuel and raged against tourists who'd steal towels and pillows from the motel units that they'd slept in for nothing while their vehicles were being repaired.

It was the perfect pace of life for a bloke who was happiest just having a chat, and he developed a special relationship with Clinton, the boy he knew as The Professor because of his insatiable curiosity. They would arm-wrestle on the bar (Clinton would always win) and go on long, slow walks up the back paddock in the evenings while Clinton pestered him about the disease that was slowly wasting his muscles.

* * *

Time passed quickly for Steve and Adele, and with few regrets. They had invested in Dunmarra with a general plan to stay for five years, enduring the strains of roadhouse life with its long hours and isolation to improve the business and sell out at a profit. But by 1993 they had bought out their business partners and had settled into a life that revolved around the daily rhythm of travel up and down the Stuart Highway. It was a stable if unspectacular business. Their competition, if they could be called competition, were the other roadhouses dotted every 90 kilometres or so in either direction; places like Daly Waters, Larrimah and Mataranka to the north and Renner Springs, Three Ways and even Wauchope to the south. Further down toward Alice Springs there were roadhouses at Wycliffe Well, Barrow Creek and Ti Tree. Each had their own history in the struggle to settle the harsh land around them, emerging over the past century as staging posts for the overland telegraph lines and placed roughly a day's ride apart on the back of a horse. When the highway was sealed and car travel became commonplace the roadhouses stayed, becoming squares on a strategy board game that a player might land upon on the 1500 kilometres between Darwin and Alice Springs.

The trip was a mathematical equation; a series of jumps of 300 kilometres or more that could be achieved in two days if necessary or a week if you had time to stop and look around at the eclectic mix of natural beauty and European persistence. The occupants of sedans and four-wheel-drives tended to prefer beds for the night in the bigger towns like Katherine or Tennant Creek, but Dunmarra was the perfect pit stop, almost exactly half-way between the two towns and a natural place to refuel and have a meal. The campervans and cars towing caravans were in less of a hurry, happy to chug along during the day and stop for the night in the middle of nowhere. It was rare that the Dunmarra campsite was empty, particularly during the tourist season in the middle of the Australian winter.

The roadhouse also benefited from its established location as a changeover point for bus drivers. There was a constant turnaround between drivers who arrived after making the haul from either Darwin or Alice Springs, slept in one of the motel units and finished their trip by taking over driving duties on the next service. The bread and butter trade came from the truckies, who were lured by three things: the size of the feed they could get in the dining room, the temperature of the beer at the bar and the standard of the service behind the counter. Dunmarra excelled at all three.

The long hours were lessened by maintaining a large staff. Julie-Ann finished school and moved back to Alice Springs, but Adele's brother Glenn and his wife Lu moved to Dunmarra from the Gold Coast in 1992 with their son Danniel who was a welcome playmate for Greg and Clinton. Steve and Adele decided that time away from the roadhouse was important. Living and working side by side could become claustrophobic so they would have three trips a year—as a family, as a couple and as individuals. Steve would go fishing with his mates up the Gulf country and Adele would busy herself with Isolated Children's Parents Association conferences. Family holidays usually meant a trip to Queensland or a long weekend in Darwin where they could enjoy what others would consider normal activities like going out to dinner with friends or the movies.

One of the biggest changes from life in Alice Springs was the weather. The family had moved more than 850 kilometres north, and the weather and landscape had changed dramatically, from the dry desert air and rocky ranges around Alice Springs to the semi-tropical heat and flat open grasslands and dense scrubby forests of the Sturt Plains. During the wet season, from December to March, Adele and the boys would sit on the front verandah watching the lightning flashes roll against the black desert skies while thunder echoed across the landscape like mortars in a war movie. The dam across the road would become a lake and yet evaporate to a cracked dirt-pan a few months later.

The boys were growing up fast, both big for their age and full of mischief. Greg was the more physical of the two and the typical older brother—dominant but ever watchful of his younger sibling. Clinton was a more complex character, devouring science books and children's encyclopaedias to devise questions he thought would flummox the adults around him.

When Adele looked at her younger son she could not help but feel especially protective. His fear of the dark had continued to be a problem;

he would wander the house late at night and often creep into her bed in the early hours of the morning because he could not bear being alone. Soon after arriving at Dunmarra she'd taken him to Melbourne to have his back teeth removed. They had rotted due to his constant demands for blackcurrant juice. Adele promised to buy him a toy as a way of taking his mind off the frightening idea of an operation and let him loose in a big city toy store. Clinton ran gleefully up and down the aisles. Able to choose anything he wanted, he came back with a plain brown teddy bear which he named Victor after his maternal grandfather because he wanted a friend beside him. After that Victor never left his side.

Nothing much seemed to happen that would unsettle the natural pace of life—at least not until the drug bust in August 1993 at the aptly named Hidden Valley station 60 kilometres to the north-west. Dunmarra was suddenly national news as the mafia was linked to a series of inland plantations worth tens of millions of dollars. In hindsight the signs should have been obvious that something was amiss, especially when the owner suddenly started paying in cash rather than credit card at the roadhouse and introduced a smooth-looking Italian as someone who was taking care of his place. It didn't add up in retrospect, but then why on earth would the Liebelts think that one of their nearest neighbours would be involved in a 10 000-plant, $20-million marijuana plantation? The crop, as it turned out, had been planted the day they celebrated their fifth anniversary at the roadhouse.

14
'Where are you going, Clint?'

Dave and Sandy Langan were on their way home to Kingaroy. After two-and-a-half years of chasing work around the top end of Australia, from Queensland through the Northern Territory and as far as Geraldton in Western Australia, the joys of a carefree itinerant working life had worn thin. The couple longed for their home town, 210 kilometres north-west of Brisbane, with its strangely comforting skyline of distinctive orange silos (to hold the region's famous peanut crops) framed by the distant green of the Bunya mountain range and national park. More to the point, they needed a period of stability; a house with wardrobes and a garden rather than a caravan, bunkhouse or swags rolled out by the side of a lonely highway. It might even be the right time to start a family if things went well.

Bonded by marriage for 10 years, both wore the stature and demeanour of hard-living country working folk—lean, strong and quietly resourceful. Work had been plentiful since they left Kingaroy in early 1991 but only because they had been prepared to be flexible. Dave, a horse handler by trade and even more so by passion, had taken jobs driving tractors and even picking tomatoes during the seasonal highs and lows of rural Australia. Like her husband, Sandy was always employable, usually finding work in the kitchen or the packing shed of the property where Dave had been given a position. His last job was a six-month stint working horses on a property outside Kununurra in northern Western Australia. Sandy had got a job as cook on a nearby tourist resort. Life was simple but fulfilling.

Part of the reason for the timing of their journey home was the delivery of two horses. One was a bay mare, Lady, which they had agreed to take to friends living in nearby Gympie. The second horse, a gift to Sandy from her employers, was a former thoroughbred racehorse; a beautiful coal black mare named Phoenix with an unremarkable country track record but bloodlines and a sound temperament that made her potential breeding stock. Phoenix was quiet as a mouse as she was led into the float in the early hours of 28 September 1993 for the 1500-kilometre trip to her new home. Sandy patted her head while Dave secured the headstall. The peaceful moment belied its importance in the chain of events that would soon unfold.

The Langans had planned a straightforward drive to Kingaroy; crossing the Western Australia–Northern Territory border on the 480-kilometre leg between Kununurra and Katherine along the Victoria Highway, then down the Stuart Highway for 600 kilometres almost as far as Tennant Creek before heading along the Barkly Highway into Queensland. Their biggest concern was the open-topped horse float and the effect of travel on the animals. It was hot, even in late spring, so the day's driving would have to be done between daybreak and 10 a.m. before making camp, breaking out their swags and spending the afternoon quietly, or perhaps riding the horses for a short time.

Luckily they were in no particular hurry. There was time to drink in the spectacular views alongside the road; the soaring escarpments, the fat-bellied boab trees and the crocodile-infested Victoria River which weaves its way through the deep valleys and gorges of the Gregory National Park. They camped just outside the town of Timber Creek, where in 1856 the explorer Augustus Charles Gregory wrecked his boat while venturing up the Victoria River in search of an inland sea that his colonial benefactors hoped existed. Gregory, who carved his arrival and departure dates into a giant boab, followed the river and its tributaries for over 500 kilometres until it disappeared into the desert sands.

It took two days to reach Katherine where they dropped the horses with people they knew and drove 300 kilometres north to Darwin for a prearranged week's holiday with Sandy's father and brother in the Kakadu National Park. It was their last fling, so to speak, before plunging back into a regular town lifestyle. On Wednesday 6 October they returned to Katherine to pick up the horses and continue on their way home to Kingaroy. It was Dave's 31st birthday the next day. They decided to try and reach Tennant Creek for the night.

As they headed down the Stuart Highway, a couple of hours outside Katherine, Dave realised he had forgotten something important. The Queensland government stock squad had to be informed about the movement of the two horses across the border. He didn't want a hassle the next day so he had to telephone the inspectorate at Mount Isa and ensure the paperwork would be ready. There was no point heading back to Katherine so he decided to pull into one of the roadhouses along the way where there was always a public phone box. It was late morning as they rounded a sweeping right-hand bend and noticed the Shell sign at Dunmarra.

Sandy thought of the horses which had been in the float for three hours: 'I'm glad we're stopping. Park on the verge and I'll take them out for a few minutes while you're on the phone. It's so bloody hot.' Dave nodded, pulling up just past the roadhouse under the eucalypts between the parking area and the bitumen, so Lady and Phoenix could be taken out away from the activity. He unlocked the float for Sandy and then walked across to the public phone box alongside the door to the dining room. Sandy was right. Not only was it hot but the humidity was claustrophobic.

The cry came as Dave began to dial: 'The horse has bolted. Dave, Dave, quick she's headed your way.' He looked up to see Phoenix clatter across the driveway and past the bowsers, and then back at the shocked look on Sandy's face as she held the empty rein. The normally placid animal had reared as a road train thundered past a few metres from the float, blaring its horn in warning. By the time he'd looked again Phoenix was in full stride, racing up the side of the highway north toward Katherine. Dave ran back to the float and jumped on Lady's back, hoping the halter would be enough to control her and catch Phoenix before she got too far away. But Lady dropped her head. By the time he got her under control Phoenix was gone. It all happened in a matter of seconds. The road train was barely a kilometre away, just topping the next hill heading south toward Alice Springs.

There was nothing they could do but secure the car and try to track down the frightened horse. The phone call was all but forgotten as they abandoned their immediate travel plans and checked into the camping ground. The horse would have to be retrieved.

The unscheduled stop to make a quick phone call would last much longer than overnight, and they would be joined in the search by hundreds, though the recovery of Phoenix would become incidental. Almost a fortnight later the couple slipped away practically unseen, their lives changed forever.

※ ※ ※

The 7 a.m. news was blaring from the radio in the roadhouse kitchen, turned up to cover the sound of the loaded breakfast grill. Adele half listened as she flipped the sizzling meat and eggs. It was the usual mix of politics and crime. Turmoil in Canberra where Prime Minister Paul Keating was fighting Aboriginal leaders over a land rights deal, and celebration in Norway where Nelson Mandela had been awarded the Nobel Peace Prize for ending apartheid. Closer to home New South Wales was gripped by the discovery of more bodies in the gruesome Backpacker Murders case and rural Victoria was bracing itself for the worst floods in a century as the Murray River threatened to burst its banks.

Floods in October? What a laugh. There'd been no rain at Dunmarra for almost eight months and the dam across the road had shrivelled to a cracked pan of red bulldust. The only news of any relevance was the German tourist who'd almost died on a bushwalk through the Kakadu National Park. The stupid bastard thought he could just set off on a nature walk through the Australian bush, and gone in by himself despite warnings by rangers that conditions were too hot. It was close to 40 degrees every day. He'd lost his food the first night, didn't know which plants he could eat and ended up living off raw lizards for three days before finding his way out again. Lucky he had water. He wouldn't have survived otherwise.

Adele turned back to the grill. She'd been up since dawn broke over the already boiling landscape. October 9 was a typically busy Saturday morning. After the breakfast crowd had continued on their way she had to load the new self-serve Coke fridges and be on hand for the weekly meat delivery. In the middle of the activity she had taken a call from Renner Springs. It was Greg Kendall, the owner of the roadhouse two hours south, who wanted to know where the boys were. She had forgotten in the rush of the week that Greg, Danniel and Clinton were supposed to be on last night's 9 p.m. bus to spend the weekend with the Kendall kids. Instead they'd gone up to Daly Waters for dinner. She and Steve made the 50-kilometre drive occasionally to enjoy a few drinks and a steak in the beer garden of the pub, just to get out of Dunmarra for a while. There wasn't much in the way of choice when you lived along the Stuart Highway. Greg was upset when he realised he'd missed out on the treat because he and Damian Kendall were good mates. Adele defused his complaints by promising to let them go the next weekend. She didn't have the time to drive them down there.

Having only three kids at Dunmarra could be difficult at times. Two would always play well together but put the third one into the mix and inevitably two would gang up against one; it was the natural order of things. Sometimes it was brothers against cousin but this morning it was the two oldest against the youngest. Clinton had given up after a while and gone off by himself, probably over in the house with Val, where she was doing the weekly clean and ironing for the family, perhaps playing with his toy cars on the chalk roads he often drew on the carport floor. Greg and Danniel were mooching around the roadhouse.

Before she knew it the morning was almost over. Steve and Glenn were getting ready to leave in the four-wheel-drive to search for the horse which had gone missing a couple of days before. It was typical of Steve. She had lost count of the number of times that her husband had stopped whatever he was doing around the roadhouse to help complete strangers with whatever problem they had at the time. It was as if he was still in the police force and felt some obligation or duty to help. The owner of the horse—David, she thought his name was—had borrowed Greg's motorbike to search across the highway but had no luck. It was horrible country out there, thick with bullwaddy and lancewood scrub. She wouldn't be surprised if the horse was never found.

Adele was chatting to a customer when Clinton stormed back in, opening the door with a series of well-placed karate kicks. The door swung back and forth violently, banging loudly against the wall and threatening to dislodge a shelf full of souvenirs. He'd been told not to do it a hundred times but either paid no attention or, more likely, simply forgot. Doors were made to be slammed and karate, even in its crudest form, was the most effective means.

'Hi Mum, can I have a drink?'

'Clinton, how many times have I told you about the door?'

'Sorry. Can I have a drink?'

'Yes, get it out of the fridge but be careful.'

As he reached into the fridge for a can of soft drink Clinton knocked over a two-litre container of milk. It soaked the four dozen cans of Coke she was about to load into the new fridge.

'Clinton, bloody hell. I told you to be careful. Get out of here. Go on, get lost.'

Clinton was gone in a flash. He wasn't going to hang around in case he ended up having to help. Adele watched him run off toward the house then turned her attention to the mess on the floor. She assumed he would jump in the car with the other kids and head off on the horse hunt. But Steve had already left, taking Greg and Danniel and assuming that Clinton was with his mother.

Val Brooks had almost finished the house when Clinton wandered back in. He'd been hanging around her feet all morning while she went about her regular Saturday morning chore, obviously at a loose end. She wasn't feeling well and the thought of the hour or so of ironing to come only made her headache worse.

'Clint, I don't feel well. I'm going to my room to lie down for a while. What are you going to do?'

'Don't know. Go over and see what Mum's doing at the roadhouse, I s'pose.'

Then he was gone, bounding out of the house with his long, skinny legs like some blond gazelle, an adventure brewing in his vivid imagination to be played out in the grounds of the complex. Val packed up the vacuum cleaner, gave the kitchen bench a quick wipe down and went to her room. She'd tackle the ironing later.

Lu Stokes was due to work the afternoon shift in the roadhouse. Like the other staff she lived in the units behind the complex. Clinton was at the bowser when she walked past. He was still wearing the t-shirt but had changed his shorts for jeans and pulled on a pair of boots.

'Aunty Lu, can you help me fill the tank?'

'Sure. Where are you going, Clint?' she replied, unscrewing the tank and noticing it was already full.

'For a ride.'

'Whereabouts?'

'Just out,' he replied vaguely, waving his arm in a sweeping motion. It could have meant anywhere behind the roadhouse where the boys had their own motocross track.

Clinton pulled on his full-faced white helmet, kick-started the bike easily and took off. Lu watched him ride off then turned and walked into the roadhouse.

15
Stay at this light

It had been a frustrating five hours in the hot bush by the time Steve and Glenn returned to the roadhouse. They'd driven around the paddock immediately to the west, across the Stuart Highway, but there was no sign of the horse; not that they had expected to find it, more a case of making the effort to help someone in trouble. Steve made for the nearest fence line of the enormous paddock, hoping the animal might have left some tracks in the clearing either side of the wire. Nothing. They tried a couple of waterholes to the south-west. No sign. The sun was still high and it was hot; uncomfortable even inside the air-conditioned cabin, and the boys were restless. They wanted something to drink and an ice-cream. It was close to 4.30 p.m. when they got back. Adele saw them from behind the counter and came out. Greg and Danniel scrambled out of the back seat and ran past her into the cool interior of the roadhouse to raid the fridge. She leaned in the back, looking for the other tousled head.

'Where's Clint? I thought he'd gone with you to help find the horse.'

Steve was puzzled. 'We didn't take him. I thought he was with you. He was hanging around the roadhouse when we left.'

Adele was a little startled, but not immediately worried. He was probably with Val, or playing out the back somewhere. 'I saw him two or three hours ago. He came in for a drink and then shot off somewhere. I haven't seen him since.'

Neither Val nor Lu had seen him since their last encounters around lunchtime, and the news that Clinton had gone off on his motorbike worried Steve. He took the car and went to search the back paddock where the boys normally rode around a track carved one day with a grader from Hayfield station. They were under strict instructions to stay within the boundaries of the paddock, which measured two square kilometres. If they ever got lost the easiest way back to safety was to follow the sun as it made its way across the sky. Steve had drummed the rule into their heads: 'The sun rises in the east and sets in the west; remember that. If you follow the sun it will bring you back to the highway.'

There was one other rule he made—never, ever cross the highway. The western side of the Stuart Highway was out of bounds if they weren't with an adult. It was not that Steve was afraid they would get hit by a passing road train; he was afraid of the consequences if one of them became lost. Steve now feared the worst. Neither Clinton nor his bike could be found behind the roadhouse. He was not in the house, nor at any of his other haunts.

Adele was in tears when he got back to the house. Dave Langan had just told her that he'd seen Clinton over the western side of the highway—the forbidden side—wrestling the chain on the gate which led to the dam and a massive paddock. Dave had spoken to Clinton and helped him shut and chain the gate. He had no idea that the boy was not supposed to be across the road, let alone on a motorbike. Val and Lu had already been searching in the area near the dam, walking the fence line and calling Clinton's name, but there was no response. Steve took Greg's motorbike and went to have a look himself. He was still not convinced that Clinton would risk going to the other side of the highway but the tyre marks in the dust by the windmill were unmistakeable. He could only surmise that Clinton had discovered he'd been left behind when they went to search for the horse, and decided to come after them.

Steve followed the trail as it headed west along the track which led to an unused bore, out toward a clutch of billabongs that formed part of the Milner Lagoon. During the wet season the billabongs joined in a six-kilometre stretch of shallow water that looked like an inland sea. But the water would gradually dry after the last rains in March, receding to a small dam which was almost dry by the end of spring. Clinton's trail ran almost three kilometres into the scrub. As Steve followed it he expected to see his son around the next corner, sheepish but relieved that someone had found him. His hopes were shattered when the tracks veered suddenly north, off the trail and into the scrub. The situation had suddenly become dire.

As soon as Adele realised Clinton had ventured west she telephoned John Dyer at Hayfield station to ask for help. Within 30 minutes their closest neighbour, 20 kilometres to the south, had arrived with two cars and seven men, including three Aboriginal trackers, who immediately mounted a search near the dam. They confirmed the sighting of Clinton with Dave Langan and picked up the motorbike track. By this time Steve had returned. The light was getting dim and the single light on Greg's tiny trailbike made it difficult to see. They headed out again, this time in the four-wheel-drives and attempted to follow the tyre marks when they turned into the bush. Eventually they were forced to give up and return to the roadhouse. It was obvious now that Clinton was lost, somewhere out there to the west in the most inhospitable scrub imaginable. Maybe he had fallen off his bike and was injured and that was why he was not answering the calls. The most pressing question was why he left the trail and headed into the bush. The obvious answer would be that he had seen the lost horse and, on a sudden impulse, tried to catch it. Steve dismissed the notion. There was no evidence of a horse in the area; no tracks other than those of cattle. The problem now was not why he had gone there but how they were going to find him.

Adele was distraught. The police had to be called. First-class Constable John White and his offsider Constable Sam Robinson manned the police station at Elliott, 104 kilometres south of Dunmarra. By chance they were at Renner Springs—the roadhouse where Clinton and his brother and cousin were supposed to be spending the weekend—when the distress call was relayed. It was now 8 p.m., well after nightfall, and it was clear that the boy would not be found until morning. Rather than rush to Dunmarra it was better to head back to Elliott and make proper plans for mounting a search at first light. By 11 p.m. the arrangements for a full aerial search and ground support had been arranged. It was too early to call Darwin for reinforcements. Resources were limited in a police force that had to cover such vast areas. The two constables headed for Dunmarra just before midnight, hoping this would not turn into a major operation. The logistics would be a nightmare.

As word began to spread Steve Liebelt barely stopped for breath. He had gone back to look around Clinton's favourite hiding places on the eastern side of the road and driven as far as the Hayfield turn-off in case Clinton had found his way back onto the highway. When it got too dark to look for tracks, he and Glenn had driven up and down the Murranji Road—a dirt road which cut through the bush in a north-westerly direction from the Stuart Highway to reach the Buchanan Highway, which began just north of Dunmarra. It roughly defined the broad search area but served only to emphasise just how big a task they faced. It was still hot and muggy at 10 p.m. as they drove the gas pipeline road—a 20-metre-wide clearing almost 10 kilometres west of Dunmarra beneath which the gas pipeline ran from Adelaide to Darwin. By daylight the clearing was obvious to anyone, even a scared little boy. If he had penetrated this far on his bike, they prayed he would have the sense to wait for help. Even if he chose to go on, and turned right or left to follow the pipeline, he would eventually stumble onto the Buchanan Highway to the north or the Murranji Road to the south. They set up lights every few hundred metres, attaching water bottles and printed notes: *Clinton. Stay at this light. There is water in the bottle.* They even attached his favourite muesli bars to make him feel as if they were close.

Adele was back at the roadhouse, manning the phones. Andy McLay called. He had hitched a lift to Katherine with a truckie the day before to go to the town's biennial race meeting and heard the news while having dinner at the pub. He would catch the morning bus to be home by lunchtime. Margie McLean, the nursing sister at Elliott, rang. She had been on call that day and been told the news by Sam Robinson. She would drive up that evening and spend the night in case Clinton was brought in. The offers were both comforting and overwhelming; a realisation that this was rapidly turning into a real, full-blown search. Why couldn't Clinton just pop out of a cupboard where he'd been hiding all this time? She tried phoning her parents every half hour but there was no answer. Where were they? Adele cried. It would be the first of many times.

Steve and Glenn had returned reluctantly from the bush by the time the police arrived that night. Clinton had been missing almost 11 hours and they knew the morning was critical. The aerial search would be considerable. John Dyer had contacted Mark Robins, a contract muster helicopter pilot who had often worked at Hayfield and knew the country well. He was at Tanambirini station, 100 kilometres north-east of Hayfield, and promised to leave the station at first light the next morning to join the search. John White had arranged with the manager of Newcastle Waters station, Ken Warriner, for three fixed-wing aircraft and observers to cover the search area at first light.

It was 2 a.m. when Adele and Steve finally got to bed. They lay in the dark, reluctant to voice the fears they both held. Steve wrestled with the notion that his son was lost simply because he had been left behind and wanted to be with his father. He had led or been a part of dozens of searches as a police officer and they had always found their targets and brought them home safely. He could not fail when it was a member of his own family. Adele knew how frightened her little Clintypops would be. He'd always been afraid of the dark, even in his own bedroom, and she couldn't imagine his level of fear out there, alone in a place that was hot even in the dead of night and there were no comforting voices. He would be running scared. She tossed and turned, unable to shake the thought. Sleep was impossible.

Debbie Bruce had been out to dinner with friends and arrived back at her Alice Springs home around midnight. Her eldest daughter, Amanda, was awake and anxious to pass on the news that Aunty Adele had called six times in the past few hours and wanted her to call as soon as she got home. It was obviously urgent and she sounded worried, Amanda insisted. Debbie looked at her watch; it was too late and she would call in the morning. Anyway, Adele was probably just on the piss and wanted to gabble. Just as she got into bed the phone rang.

It was Adele. 'Debbie, Clinton is lost.' The words cut through Debbie like a knife. 'What do you mean lost? How could he be lost?'

Adele tearfully repeated the story about Steve and the boys looking for the lost horse and Clinton going after them. With each new twist Debbie became steadily more worried. She could hear the rising fear in her best friend's voice and it was unsettling. Adele was always the calm one. Nothing ever seemed to faze her, so why was she so stressed now? Debbie could not comprehend what the word 'lost' meant. How could a child be lost from his own home? How could he be lost in the bush and not see the lights of Dunmarra and just follow them home?

She didn't know what to say, other than to talk about Greg in the hope that it would take Adele's mind off Clinton and stop the panic that was obviously setting in. They talked for a while longer until Adele said she needed to get off the phone. Something was happening. She would call back in an hour.

Debbie was shattered. Nothing made sense but her friend was hurting and she had to do something. She felt useless; no help at all trying to assure Adele there was nothing to worry about. Of course there was—her son was out there alone.

Shenandoah: The search begins

Adele woke with a start. She bolted upright, ignoring her raw eyes and dry mouth. It had been a short, shallow, fitful sleep. Was it all a dream? She struggled to recall putting Clinton to bed last night. She looked around the strewn sheets to see if he had crept into the room, as he often did, but he wasn't there. Neither was Steve. The men were already drawing up plans in the roadhouse when she walked in a few minutes later. It was just after 4 a.m. and still pitch black outside. Adele shuddered with the notion that her little boy was out there somewhere, alone and terribly frightened. She went to help make breakfast, hoping the activity would take her mind off the gut-wrenching thought, but she felt sick at the sight of food.

John Dyer was briefing police and searchers about the type of terrain they were about to face. It was his land out there. He had owned it since 1971 when he quit his job as an Elders stock agent and struck out on his own. The paddock into which Clinton had disappeared was at the back of the property he called Shenandoah—the western half of Hayfield. The land was only used for grazing; it was good for nothing else. In fact, he'd just finished mustering almost 400 head which had been in there for most of the year. The grazing was fine during and just after the wet season because there was plenty of water, but not now. It was full of bullwaddy, lancewood and turpentine; the scrub was impenetrable in many parts, even for cattle. Access for the four-wheel-drives would be difficult at best and impossible in many parts.

The key to finding Clinton quickly, before dehydration set in, would be aerial searches. They had three fixed-wing aircraft and at least two helicopters at their disposal which would be used in a meticulous grid pattern, flying back and forth across set compass readings so the ground was covered as carefully, but as quickly, as possible. On the ground they had 20 four-wheel-drives, three motorbikes and five horses which would match the process and be ready to move to any area nominated by the pilots and their observers.

The bottom line, Dyer told them gravely, was that they probably only had until late in the afternoon to find the boy alive. The ground temperature soared well into the high forties each day, there was no visible surface water and Clinton had taken no supplies. His chances of survival were slim at best. The starting point would be to find the tracks they had lost in the dark the previous night. Steve and John White would take the three Aboriginal trackers from Hayfield—Dennis Neade, Charlie Chungaloo and Patrick Cutta—out past the dam where Steve had found Clinton's tracks. The aerial grid search would begin at first light.

It took only a few minutes to find the tracks which they followed west until staking all four tyres of their vehicle on the unforgiving groundcover. They continued the search on foot, slowly picking their way through thick timber in the grey dawn and then scouring a clearing of hard-packed ground where they would have lost the signs if not for the skills of the trackers.

As promised, Mark Robins arrived from Tanambirini station at 6.30 a.m. He barely knew the Liebelts, and the call for help had come while the mustering season was still in full swing, but he didn't hesitate. When asked later he would reply, simply: 'They needed a helicopter and I was there to do a job as best I could. If it was my kid out in the bush I would expect the same sort of help, so you give what you expect of other people.' It echoed the feelings of hundreds who would join him over the next few days, including three colleagues—Steve Stanley, Bob Christianson and Sam Borg—who were among the 20 pilots employed by Helimuster, a company which hired out choppers and pilots for mustering and mineral survey work. The company operated out of Victoria River Downs station, more than 300 kilometres to the northwest.

Mark and John Dyer took off almost immediately to join the three fixed-wing aircrafts which had flown over from Newcastle Waters and were working patterns to the south and north-west. They flew over the ground search party led by Steve Liebelt, picking up the tracks on the other side of the clearing and working their way ahead of the men on foot. It was painfully slow progress, even from the air, as the evidence of Clinton's path appeared and then disappeared as he wound his way through the scrub. At one stage he had been stymied by an old fence. Instead of turning back, Clinton had ridden up and down the rusting wire until he found a way to get past. It appeared that the only constant was that he was heading west, away from safety.

Suddenly John spotted it. The bright yellow and blue motorbike was half-hidden in a patch of spear grass which stood almost as high as the machine itself. It was hard to keep their excitement under control as they landed. Clinton had to be nearby; the job was over, he was safe. But as the minutes ticked by and his tousled blond head did not appear from the nearby trees to greet them, it dawned on them that the boy was gone.

There was no radio contact with those below so while Mark searched the surrounding bush John set out on foot to get the others, including Steve Liebelt, who were a kilometre behind and tiring as the ground temperature rose. It was mixed news—the excitement of a breakthrough tainted with the fear that Clinton was in more serious trouble than they'd imagined. He'd ignored or forgotten another lesson that Steve had repeated ad nauseum to the boys, the first law in bush survival—to never leave their bikes if they got lost or had an accident.

Steve was distraught by the time he reached the bike. He tried hard to remain positive as he almost ran the last few hundred metres to the clearing. Maybe Clint was sleeping nearby, a little the worse for wear from a night in the bush but otherwise unhurt. God, he hoped so. The big man checked the bike before rushing to the far side of the clearing to call, in the desperate hope that Clinton had not strayed far from his machine. There was no answer.

The bike was upright on its stand, four kilometres out from the roadhouse with the fuel tank still half full. The fuel tap was on and the light switched off. Steve cast his eyes around the clearing, looking for reasons why Clinton might have abandoned the machine. The area around it looked like a lunar landscape, rutted with deep crevices that made it almost impassable for a vehicle. The locals called them crab holes and it looked as if Clinton had plunged into one as he worked his way through the scrub. The right-hand brake lever was bent almost at 90 degrees. The throttle on the same handlebar was difficult to turn. It took several attempts to start the bike. Steve could only guess, but it looked as though the bike might not have started for Clinton because the fuel was vaporising between the carburettor and the combustion chamber. It was a common enough problem with little two-stroke motors once they got too hot. An adult would have known that the engine needed to cool down before trying again but, despite his inquisitive maturity, Clinton was still an eight-year-old boy.

Clinton's state of mind seemed obvious from the muddle of boot prints around the bike—size five R.M. Williams riding boots with the longhorn logo on the rubber heel. It removed any doubt—if any had existed—that he was unsure what to do next. There must have been some hesitation, perhaps remembering his father's instructions about leaving the machine, but in the end inexperience and a lack of fear of the bush won out.

The boot prints headed north-west. The men followed as quickly as possible, easing their way through dense strands of lancewood, sometimes crawling through thickets that contained nothing but thick blankets of spiderweb. The silence was palpable; there were no birds in these trees. Nothing seemed to live here. The explorer John Stuart had encountered these vast stands of trees in 1861. His party had turned back twice before finding a way past the area that would later become Dunmarra.

The trail ran for almost two kilometres before it was lost as the sun reached its peak and the temperature galloped past 40 degrees. John Dyer and Mark Robins had continued their grid search from above. As the trail ran out below they decided to head back to Dunmarra, refuel and bring out fresh tyres for the abandoned four-wheel-drive. Steve, John White and the trackers headed back to the car to wait, and to pray they were not too late.

Back at the roadhouse the activity had been non-stop. People and machinery were arriving as fast as police could send them off in small teams. Nine Aboriginal trackers who had driven up from Elliott's

Gurungu community during the morning were sent out to the gas pipeline road 10 kilometres to the west. While the aerial and ground searches concentrated on an area almost five kilometres back toward the roadhouse, their job was to look for any sign that Clinton had reached, and perhaps crossed, the pipeline. If the search area was wrong then they would have to move quickly but it seemed unlikely that the boy would have penetrated this far into the bush, especially now that he was on foot. The trackers walked eight kilometres along the pipeline, scouring the ground on both sides, but found no sign of a footprint in the baked surface.

When police officer John White got back to the roadhouse he was told there were almost 100 people waiting patiently by the side of the Stuart Highway at the Buchanan Highway turn-off, eight kilometres north of Dunmarra. There were RAAF personnel from the Tindal base outside Katherine, an army reserve unit which had been on its way back to Sydney but stopped to help out, a growing group of Northern Territory Emergency Services (NTES) personnel, distinct in their bright orange overalls, and dozens of volunteers from town who had dropped what they were doing when they heard the news and driven down to help. Constable White was stunned. He briefed the group and bussed them three kilometres along the Buchanan where they lined up, an arm's width apart, and formed a human chain to walk into the bush in the first mass ground grid search. It would take three hours to walk just two kilometres.

The aerial search team had also grown. Bob Christianson and Steve Stanley had flown across from Victoria River Downs and were helping to set grid lines for the increasing number of teams on the ground. The gas pipeline road seemed to have become the physical and psychological boundary to the search, as if they had defined the pen in which Clinton was roaming and it was just a matter of cornering him.

After delivering fresh tyres to the stranded four-wheel-drive Mark Robins and John Dyer expanded their search area. It was obvious that Clinton had moved further west but searching was becoming more difficult in the increasingly hostile terrain. When they found a place to land, the pair would set out on foot in opposite directions for 20 minutes, hoping to pick up his tracks. Navigation on the ground was next to impossible because the featureless landscape was dense with bush, so the helicopter's engine was left running so they could *hear* their way back to safety. Their persistence paid off. In a clearing four kilometres west of the motorbike John spotted a boot print left as Clinton pushed his way through a thicket of lancewood. It was a tantalising clue but an hour in the area failed to find anything more. They needed more help; fresh eyes in case something had been missed. Better still, a tracker's eyes.

Rob Teague was the head stockman at Humbert River station, west of Victoria River Downs. The 23-year-old had arrived that morning with a team of ringers and Aboriginal trackers; he had been at a bush stock camp preparing for a muster when they were diverted to help the search. There was no argument from the eight blokes he brought with him. They all knew the Liebelt family, at least by sight, because Dunmarra was one of the places they liked to have a drink and let their hair down if they were travelling between Humbert River and its sister station, Newcastle Waters. Rob's fiancée, Michelle, was also with the team, travelling as their cook. She had been a governess at Hayfield station next door a year or so before and had got to know Clinton and Greg very well. Their efforts to help would be personal.

They had spent the day working their way through the bush back toward the roadhouse from the gas pipeline road. As they rested the horses in the late afternoon the call came in that Rob and his senior tracker, Noely Campbell, were needed to check out a set of prints several kilometres to the south. While the rest of his team continued their search, Rob and Noely were picked up by chopper and dropped into the clearing where the motorbike still stood—a lonely sight with dozens, maybe a hundred or more people spread out trying to find its rider.

They studied the scene, trying to gauge what could have happened 24 hours earlier. Finding the machine upright on its stand suggested that Clinton might have had a reason to stop other than an accident. Maybe the boy had found the lost horse and tried to catch it, they pondered. The scuffle of boot prints clearly visible around the clearing looked as if they could have been made by someone shifting from side to side, as if trying to herd and block the animal into a corner. When the horse got away from his youthful efforts Clinton must have blithely followed it into the bush. In an instant he would have lost sight of his bike and all sense of direction.

The tracks Rob and Noely followed from the clearing told a much clearer story. At first the boot prints were flat—weight evenly distributed across the foot—as Clinton made his way through the bush to a cattle pad where he turned west, probably believing he was heading toward Dunmarra. Two kilometres further on the situation changed dramatically. The boot prints suddenly shortened, Clinton's toes digging into the soft sand as he had begun to trot, then jog and finally run in growing panic as he realised that night was setting in. About the same time Steve and Adele were first raising the alarm and beginning to search his favourite hiding places on the eastern side of the highway at the back of the roadhouse, Clinton was running as fast as he could west, away from the roadhouse, following the sun—just like Dad told him.

※ ※ ※

Steve Liebelt's old CIB boss, Trevor Green, was agitated. He was convinced that the local police weren't reacting quickly enough to the emerging crisis at Dunmarra, but he couldn't do a damn thing about it. It was not that Trevor was critical of the Elliott police, more the bureaucratic dilemma they and other remote area police faced when an emergency occurred. Should they act swiftly and call in as many people as soon as possible or wait, in case the situation was not as serious as first thought and became a waste of money and resources? Like most organisations of its type the police force was often hampered because of the need to be cost-conscious, and the mentality was pushed down through the ranks. Because of the isolation of Dunmarra and its lack of infrastructure, the Elliott police were wary about crying wolf and asking for a massive response to something that might be resolved within half an hour.

Trevor had no doubt about what had to be done. The task force—the specialist manhunt police unit—should have been called in by late Saturday afternoon, when it became obvious that the boy was indeed lost and not just hiding. Trevor's experience told him that the first 24 hours were the most critical of any investigation—be it a lost child or murder. Beyond that timeframe, there was a danger that the investigation would falter.

Steve Liebelt had called him on Saturday evening, then again on Sunday morning. His friend and former colleague desperately needed help, yet here he was sitting in a bloody office in Darwin, unable to break the bonds of officialdom.

It wasn't until 1.30 p.m. on Sunday—a full day after Clinton's disappearance—that a small unit of seven task force officers under the command of Sergeant John Smith was dispatched. They would not arrive at Dunmarra until close to midnight.

Trevor Green faced another problem. He desperately wanted to go to Dunmarra himself, if only to support his mate. His superiors had refused permission, fearing he would interfere with the official search, pull rank on the search command team which was being put in place. There was a fine line between being a police officer and a private citizen and Trevor was straddling it.

※ ※ ※

The day had dragged through a series of peaks and cavernous troughs for Adele. There had been great excitement around midday when the call came in that Clinton's motorbike had been found. The discovery had been as swift as everyone had hoped and, like the men at the scene, those gathered in the dining room expected it to be followed almost immediately by the triumphant news of Clinton's rescue. Communications had been frustrated all morning by radio problems. The helicopters and ground team were on different radio frequencies and thus forced to relay their progress via Hayfield station from where Val Dyer would phone the roadhouse to pass on the news.

Adele's mood darkened as the silent minutes dragged into hours. She could do nothing but wait, listening for the helicopters as they returned every hour for fuel, rushing outside in the hope she would spy a small hand waving furiously from the front seat. But each time she was left feeling empty. The only news drifting in was that more footprints had been found; nothing else. Greg was being irritating, getting under everyone's feet, showing off and being cheekier than usual. She quickly realised that these were the reactions of a 10-year-old struggling to cope with his surreal surroundings.

The phone rang incessantly; friends, family, even strangers, with offers of help. Clinton's teacher, Allen Eade, called to say he would be arriving in the evening and that other KSA staff would follow tomorrow. Patricia Stokes called every hour—still guilty that she and Vic had been out dancing the previous night and missed their daughter's desperate calls. They were booked on a flight and would be at Dunmarra the next day; Debbie Bruce and Peter Kerr would collect them at Alice Springs airport and drive them up. Adele's brother Kim called twice, unsure if he should come over from Toowoomba. It was a three-day drive under normal circumstances but he and his wife Lin could do it in just over a day if they took turns. Adele told him to wait.

Janelle and Reg Underwood had arrived from Bunda station. Adele had called them the previous night when Clinton had first gone missing and earlier that day when his bike was found. 'I'll ring you back in a couple of hours when we've found him,' she told her friend confidently. By early afternoon there was still no news and Janelle could wait no longer. The couple flew across in their Cessna 172 that afternoon with clothes to last two days. They would stay for a week, swagging outside next to the tiny plane.

While Janelle joined the growing cluster of women around Adele at the roadhouse, Reg would use his plane as aerial support for the helicopters, flying above them at around 150 metres, not only searching for Clinton but also keeping an eye on the ground search teams. Reg was part of the crucial network, ensuring that the search for one person did not become an emergency for many more. The police turned a blind eye to the use of the Stuart Highway as a landing strip.

When she wasn't on the phone Adele wandered the complex in a daze, her mind a tangle of thoughts and fears. She shuddered at the thought of what she had said to Clinton the previous morning, jokingly telling him to 'get lost', and prayed they would not be the last words she spoke to him. The driveway baked in the mid-afternoon sun. As she turned to walk back inside, out of the heat, Adele gazed across the highway past the silent bore windmill and whispered the simple question that everyone was asking—'Clinton, where are you?'

Adele could not keep count of the people who kept arriving. There seemed to be hundreds, many of them in uniform, others she recognised as townspeople from Katherine and other small communities—Larrimah, Mataranka, Elliott, even Tennant Creek. Some she'd never seen before. Where were they all from? As night fell Adele watched Steve come in with the rest of the growing search team. He looked terrible, shattered; and her heart broke again, this time for a father who could not find his son. They embraced, words useless as they wept for their son and themselves.

Outside the search continued throughout the night. Teams of vehicles patrolled the gas pipeline road and the Buchanan Highway in the hope that their lights and sirens would give Clinton some beacon of hope in his second night alone in the bush. Adele couldn't bring herself to sleep inside the house, not while Clinton was out in the bush. Eventually she succumbed to the urging of others, rolled out Clinton's swag in the dining room and lay down next to Allen Eade, who'd arrived just before midnight with his girlfriend. It was 3 a.m. and she was exhausted, but there would be no sleep for her.

17
Don't give up hope

It was daybreak on Monday when Peter Kerr, Debbie Bruce and Adele's parents pulled into Dunmarra. Peter and Debbie had taken turns driving through the night from Alice Springs. The news of Clinton's disappearance had shocked and confused all the family's friends living in and around Alice Springs. The notion that he was lost was hard to grasp; it was as if they had to be convinced it was true. Peter understood intuitively the crisis they were facing. It was difficult enough for an adult to survive in the bush around Alice Springs for a few days, let alone a child in that godforsaken scrub around Dunmarra.

It had been a tough journey, psychologically; two of the people closest to Steve and Adele, Clinton's godfather and Adele's best friend, both with children the same age as Clinton, struggling with their own fears and emotions while trying to make conversations with his worried grandparents. Patricia Stokes kept telling the story of how Adele had been lost on the beach at a Welsh seaside resort when she was five years old, to be eventually found by Patricia's best friend, happily unaware of the drama around her. Debbie was sure Patricia believed that history would repeat itself and Adele's best friend would simply walk into the bush and find Clinton. Or maybe Debbie expected it of herself. Either way, she clung to the hope that Adele would be waiting when they arrived with a smile on her face and the reassuring words: 'It's okay they've found him.'

The reality was frightening. Debbie stared in horror at the activity before her—buses, cars and people everywhere; police task force in dark blue, army in camouflage khaki and NTES volunteers in bright orange. This was not what she had expected, and Adele's face as she came to meet them was etched with fear. There were no words of reassurance; Clinton was indeed lost. The heat smothered the landscape like a blanket, even at dawn, as they watched two coaches pull out of the roadhouse packed with 100 or more volunteers who would spend the day carefully combing bushland between the gas pipeline road and the Stuart Highway.

Adele led her best friend and her parents to the house, past the crowds waiting to be dispersed into the wilderness, to go over the story again and again as if doing so would make some sense of it. There was none; no logical explanation, no blame, for the chain of events and the crisis that was unfolding.

The fax machine inside the cluttered roadhouse office was running constantly, churning out messages of support and offers of help as word spread across the Territory. From Jindare station, far to the north, came the promise of six men: 'Six volunteer walkers enroute to Dunmarra. ETA 3.30–4 a.m. (possibly earlier). All fit men. Our thoughts and prayers go with them to you.' Other stations followed suit, their names spitting out from the machine like a call of the alphabet—Auvergne, Balbarini, Beetaloo, Bradshaw, Camfield, Elkedra, Erldunda, Hamilton Downs, Helen Springs, Henbury, Hodgeson River, Humbert River, Inverway, Lamboo, Legune, Maryfield, Mataranka, Montejini, Mount Cavanagh, Numery, Scott Creek, Sunday Creek, Tanambirini, Victory Downs, Walhallow, Wave Hill, Willaroo.

Most of the staff from the Katherine School of the Air had become involved, either joining the ground search or helping in the kitchen. Bureaucratic approval for their action went as high as the deputy secretary in Darwin. The few teachers left in Katherine doubled and tripled up on radio lessons to cover for their colleagues, as well as managing constant telephone calls from concerned station families across the Territory. After lessons were finished for the day, the school used the radio service to provide updates on the search. Even the school's four vehicles were ferrying people and supplies between Katherine and Dunmarra.

Others simply offered hope, like Jenny and Keith Oliver at the Keep River National Park, almost 700 kilometres north-west by road, whose children John, Lisa and Terry added their own voices. Terry was a playmate of Clinton's and was sure his friend would be found safely: 'Clinton is such a true sports kid he'll make it home. You don't have to worry because Clint knows his way around. He'll soon get home to you. I can't think of what to say. He's a great buddy. We play a lot at camp. I have been asking God to bring him safely home to you. Don't give up hope.'

The scene inside the roadhouse was chaotic; a constant stream of activity. The police task force had taken over the dining room as their command centre and the army had taken over the kitchen. There were now more than 300 searchers on the ground, and air support had increased with the arrival of another two helicopters, including the Lloyds Search and Rescue helicopter which brought a doctor and two tracker dogs from the RAAF base at Tindal. They would be followed by 50 army personnel from the base, a self-sufficient group that set up an outside kitchen to supply meals around the clock, and over 100 extra volunteers from NTES.

Vic Stokes and Peter Kerr wanted to get out into the bush and help search. So did Val Brooks. She and a few other Dunmarra staff members had gone out for an hour the previous evening and she was desperate to be part of the effort to find the boy she knew and loved so much. She and Adele decided to shut down the schoolroom: 'They [Greg and Danniel] would be no good doing school work anyway.'

* * *

The bush was harsher than Val could ever have imagined. Pushing her way into it, only a few metres from the edge of the road she couldn't see where she'd just come from. Vic Stokes was barely an arm's length away from her but she could only hear his voice calling out for Clinton. Most people think of the outback as a desert but it's not all like that—this was a dry, mean forest—fields of arrow-straight lancewoods so close together that you had to squeeze between them, and thickets of ugly bullwaddy spreading their angry branches as if to block your path at every turn. Stands of turpentine soared above them but little grew beneath in the cement-hard earth where groundcover consisted largely of spinifex and kerosene grass; the latter earning its name because it smelled like the fuel when it burned. Bird life was limited to tiny foragers like the hardy grey-crowned babbler, apostle birds and hooded robins. Animal life was even less apparent; only the spectacled hare-wallaby and northern nailtail wallaby found shelter here.

Val and the others continuously called out Clinton's name, as if the volume of friendly voices would be enough to bring him scurrying out from behind the next tree like some naughty boy who had tricked them all. The bushes were thick with the webs of the golden orb spider, and the air was choked with dust kicked up from packed red earth that had last felt rain almost eight months before. The heat was horrendous. She was thirsty already.

The grid searches were designed like a giant human broom, meticulously combing the dense scrubland; the searchers crawled under bushes, climbed among the branches of bullwaddy and turpentine and risked snakebite by raking through spinifex grass that sometimes grew as high as their heads. When the grid reached the target compass point, the line of searchers would shift single file past a designated endpoint, line up again facing in the opposite direction and move back toward the starting point. It was slow, uncomfortable work. Val's group was making its way south from the Buchanan Highway, walking into the bush for almost two kilometres and then shifting to the west and walking north back to the highway. The optimism of the first half hour had drained by the time they sat down on the verge around 1 p.m. for something to eat and drink. To Val the task now seemed impossible. But they had to keep going.

The afternoon continued the same way until Val fell. She didn't know why; whether she had tripped or just collapsed. She wasn't hurt but something inside snapped and she began crying, great uncontrollable sobs of guilt and devastation. She tried to explain herself as people gathered around to see if she was injured—that she was Clinton's governess: 'I'm his teacher, I'm Clint's teacher.' But no-one seemed to understand the special bond.

The search leader decided she should be evacuated and called for a helicopter. Vic Stokes would go back as well, exhausted after the overnight journey from Queensland. As they sat in the chopper, its doors removed so searchers could see better, Val forced herself to look down.

She was afraid of heights but wanted to see the search area from the air. As soon as she did, Val thought how hopeless it was—a canopy of green tree tops, no space between them where Clinton might be visible.

Elders' agent Greg Henckel heard the helicopter which took Val Brooks back to the roadhouse. The choppers had been buzzing overhead all day, making him feel as though he was in the middle of a war movie. The only thing missing was the gunfire. The grim mind-joke took his thoughts off his feet, blistering in the normally comfortable workboots he wore each day in the stockyards around Katherine. He'd reached for them instinctively when he threw on jeans and a long-sleeved shirt to join 40 other townspeople on board an army bus just after midnight in response to the first call for volunteers to help find Clinton Liebelt. Now he wished he had chosen a pair of sandshoes.

The mood had been subdued as the volunteers, including three workmates from Elders—Peter Moffat, Bruce Cameron and Andy Gray—settled on the bus for a four-hour ride that would get them to the roadhouse just before dawn, in time for a quick feed before heading out into the bush. As Greg looked around the bus he realised that most of the faces were familiar, even if the names didn't spring readily to mind. That was the way of the outback; the Liebelts lived 300 kilometres away but people had reacted to the call for help as if they were next-door neighbours or family. The nervous chatter died instantly when an army officer sitting at the front of the bus rose to his feet. 'Look, it's going to be hot out there and it's probably going to be unpleasant so the smartest thing we can all do is to stop talking and try and get some sleep.' It wasn't a lecture but a warning that this was not an adventure to be savoured but an ordeal to be endured. The lights went out and Greg had tried to sleep, his head filled with thoughts and fears of what lay ahead.

The soldier had been right. By mid-afternoon Greg's feet were burning so badly he could barely walk, and the backs of his eyelids felt as if someone had rubbed them with sandpaper. Neither he nor his search partners had any idea where they had searched or how far they had walked in this meaningless terrain. The physical discomfort was aggravated by the emotional trauma. Greg wondered how he would cope in this bush as an adult, let alone an eight-year-old boy who must have been shit-scared the moment he realised he was lost. Greg thought about how he would react to finding the child's body and desperately hoped that someone else would find him.

No-one did. The afternoon ended forlornly. Back at the roadhouse Greg slumped beneath the dartboard and drained two stubbies to wash away the dust. He had to go back to Katherine that night. He didn't know how to feel—thankful to be going home to a shower, a good night's sleep, an ordinary day's work, or ashamed that he was leaving while others stayed to help. As he stood to leave Greg noticed that Steve Liebelt had come in. He had been out since first light searching in vain for his son and was now circling the room, quietly comforting the men and women who had come to help him. Greg left, determined to return later in the week.

※ ※ ※

Superintendent Col Hardman surveyed the frenetic activity below as the pilot of the small plane looked for a place to land. It was 1 p.m. on Monday and the side of the Stuart Highway looked more like a giant car yard than a desert highway, with trucks, cars and even road trains parked along its eastern verge for hundreds of metres either side of the Dunmarra roadhouse. Hardman could see the helicopters and fixed-wing aircraft working out to the west, and even though the bulk of the search team was out in the bush there were still dozens of people moving in and out of the roadhouse on the various errands associated with such a massive operation.

The search for Clinton Liebelt was no ordinary situation, and that was exactly why Hardman, the head of the force's special operations unit, had been sent to take over command. The task had become too big for local police to handle and needed a firm management hand—and an accompanying senior rank to avoid arguments—to ensure it did not turn into a free-for-all. There were already problems, with one cowboy from Katherine running amuck overnight, taking his four-wheel-drive across the very bush tracks on which the searchers had hoped to find prints. There was also concern that the overwhelming generosity of the local community had become just that—overwhelming. They now had more than enough people; the last thing they needed was to end up searching for lost volunteers as well as Clinton. The biggest difficulty was that because of Dunmarra's isolation the search had to be conducted from the roadhouse rather than an office away from the grieving family.

Hardman had plenty of experience to draw upon. Like Trevor Green, he had joined the Northern Territory force from Victoria. Over the past 23 years his career had taken him from one side of the Territory to the other—from bush stations in the Tanami Desert in the west to Avon Downs to the east—to a nine-year stint in Alice Springs and now Darwin and upper management level. Hardman also knew Steve Liebelt. Not only were they colleagues in the force but had played against one another in the Alice Springs Football League back in the seventies when Steve was a rangy ruckman for Rovers and Hardman a key forward for Federals.

Their professional relationship and personal friendship would prove something of a double-edged sword for Hardman. Steve Liebelt understood the realities of the way the search had to be conducted, and despite the emotion-charged atmosphere of the roadhouse was likely to back Hardman's decisions. He hoped they would be the right ones.

* * *

By mid-afternoon Steve Stanley was becoming agitated. The normally affable pilot was nursing a sore back after curling his 190-centimetre frame inside the cramped cockpit of his Japanese-designed Kawasaki helicopter for more than 20 hours. His discomfort was exacerbated by the frustration of not finding any sign of Clinton Liebelt as he and Mark Robins combed the terrain between the Stuart Highway and the gas pipeline. Steve had been over the area just two days before the search began; he and a stock inspector had swept the paddock for three hours to flush out any stray cattle left behind in the muster ordered by John Dyer. They had found nothing then, but the fleet of choppers which now hovered over Dunmarra had flushed out at least five bullocks as well as rubbish left strewn in the bush by the search teams. How could they miss the boy? Either he was hiding because he was afraid of the choppers, in which case there was no way they would be able to spot him among the trees, or they were looking in the wrong place.

Mark Robins agreed, his own frustrations growing as the hours passed. As they finished the last pass of their search grid the two pilots landed their machines to take a rest and discuss whether they should break with the main strategy and cross the western edge of the search boundary—the gas pipeline road. Mark had the same feeling as Steve—the search had to move west and quickly. Time was running out on two counts: there were only three hours of daylight left, and it was now more than two days since Clinton was last seen. Most of the station people reckoned 48 hours was about the limit for anyone out here without food and water. They decided to take a chance and trust their own instincts.

As the sun began to dip toward the horizon, the choppers crossed to the western side of the gas pipeline road and headed to a creek bed known as Kings Pond, which filled during the wet season but had been bone dry for months. It seemed an obvious place to start, the best place to spot tracks if there were any to be found. Steve landed and sat in the cockpit, letting the motor cool down while his spotter, local Mataranka copper Murray Taylor, began scouring the shallow, tree-lined banks. He had just unstrapped his seat belt when Murray shouted. He had found a set of footprints.

Steve's heart was in his mouth. He'd been right; the pipeline road hadn't stopped Clinton at all. He probably crossed it in the middle of the night, maybe even before the search teams came through with their strobe lights and signs. There was no way of knowing why, only that Clinton was now far further west than anyone had imagined. He radioed Mark who had landed a few hundred metres behind. The prints were clear, precise. Typical bush kid; he'd taken off his boots to walk in the soft sand. The tracks followed the creek as it wound its way north-west. If they leap-frogged up the creek bed they might get to Clinton before nightfall. Mark flew back three kilometres to find Rob Teague's ground party, including trackers Noely Campbell and Johnny Devlin, which had been carefully following the boy's boot prints all day. Their find had to be authenticated before the Dunmarra command centre was notified.

John Dyer was back at Dunmarra when Steve's radio report came in and jumped in with Victoria River Downs pilot, Sam Borg, who was refuelling. They crossed to the north of the creek bed, past the other two choppers making their way along it, and began a grid search from east to west. Just before 4 p.m. John spotted a pair of jeans a kilometre to the north-west of the footprints. They were now almost eight kilometres west of the motorbike and over 12 kilometres from Dunmarra. Again the trackers, who had lost Clinton's tracks after he left the creek bed, were brought in but could find no footprints. They were pulled out soon after so RAAF sniffer dogs could be brought in. The signs were bad. If Clinton was starting to take off his clothes it was a clear indication that dehydration had set in and he was beginning to hallucinate.

18
A community comes together

Margie McLean had experienced some gut-wrenching moments in her two decades as a Territory nurse. Death was a constant by-product of the harsh environment in which she chose to ply her trade, whether the consequence of the constant stream of car accidents along the Stuart Highway or as she had once witnessed, the result of an Aboriginal mother of four abandoning her youngest in the bush because he was sickly. They all left their mark on a woman who first came to the Territory from Victoria in 1970 when the population of Darwin was 30 000 and radio telephone was the only means of communication from the remote cattle stations like Victoria River Downs where she settled. Her plan had been to bide her time until she could get a Community Aid Abroad posting to the Solomon Islands. Instead, she fell in love with the frontier spirit of the northern settlers and the spirituality of its traditional people, and chose to stay.

Now in her mid-forties, Margie had married a local stockman and raised two children. For the past eight years she had been based in Elliott, running a community health care office with another nurse and five Aboriginal healthcare workers. Their patch covered 30 000 square kilometres between Daly Waters and Renner Springs, where they were the mainstay of the physical and emotional health of the scattered population, both black and white.

Of all her experiences in remote-area nursing, nothing had prepared her for the Dunmarra search. Harrowing was the way she would describe it in the years to come. Margie had driven to Dunmarra when Sam Robinson had called on Saturday night because she was worried about Adele's emotional state rather than Clinton's physical safety.

She had packed an overnight bag just in case there were complications and she had to stay, wrote husband Lindsay a note to say where she'd gone and left in the four-wheel-drive. It didn't occur to her to take the ambulance; that would have seemed a bit dramatic for a situation that would probably take three or four hours to resolve.

But that situation had altered dramatically over the next 48 hours as the boy's plight worsened and the continuing arrival of police and army personnel, emergency workers, station staff and civilian volunteers turned the roadhouse into a virtual town. It had become a crisis not only in terms of finding Clinton Liebelt, but in managing the health and welfare of the huge number of volunteers. There would undoubtedly be casualties among the searchers, if only because of the stifling heat. Margie transformed one of the tiny motel units into a clinic, with three single beds and a dresser lined with drugs and bandages where she treated searchers for everything from sunburn and dehydration to cuts, bruises and sprained ankles. She hammered nails into the walls to store IV drips and used the overnight Greyhound bus service to ferry supplies from Tennant Creek and Katherine.

There would be more than 260 patients before the search was over, many badly sunburned or complaining of cramps and dizziness, which she dealt with by giving them a salt supplement dissolved in water. Others were experiencing nausea from sheer exhaustion and would have to sip rehydration salts or, if the vomiting was too bad, face an injection. At least a dozen were so dehydrated they needed an IV drip. Three were evacuated to hospital in Katherine. There were allergic reactions to mosquitoes and sandflies. Some searchers developed chest infections and colds from the stress and tension. Twisted ankles were common, as were eye injuries, from pushing through the tough scrub. When she was not treating patients Margie was filling large plastic bottles with a diluted mixture of rehydration salts to be dropped into the search lines by helicopter.

By Monday afternoon as the search progressed without any sign of Clinton, the question became whether he was going to be found alive. The boy had been alone in the sweltering bush without food or water for more than two days. If he was still alive then it was medically improbable he could survive much longer. Margie would have to find a way to explain the truth to Adele.

The news that John Dyer and Sam Borg had found Clinton's jeans gave her the excuse she needed to broach the subject of what condition the boy might be in—alive or dead. She and Adele were on standby to be flown to the site when he was eventually found. Expectation hung in the air as they stood waiting on the verandah of the roadhouse amid a cluster of exhausted searchers who had just returned from the main search site. Margie didn't want to let the opportunity pass: 'I know it's hard to bear, but you shouldn't expect Clinton to be in the same condition as when he went out there.'

Adele nodded slowly. She knew he would be in a bad way when they found him: 'I know. I'm worried about what they'll find.'

Margie persisted: 'Well, heat does some strange things. If he's been sitting under a tree then we could be dealing with sunburn and some pretty severe dehydration. It might even mean rehydrating him with an injection.'

'What if he didn't take cover?'

'I don't know. He would probably be delirious, maybe in a coma. His kidneys may be affected. It's impossible to know, we can only guess, but you must prepare yourself for the worst.'

'I know, I know. God I hope they find him soon.'

The conversation petered out. The point had been made. The wait resumed as the shadows lengthened across the driveway. It was now just after 6 p.m. and time was running out if they were going to find Clinton before the light ran out. A police officer Margie knew as Joe Smith emerged from the dining room and strode quickly toward her, face unreadable. Something had happened. They'd found Clinton? The search was over?

'There's been an accident. One of the choppers has gone down. I'm sorry, but the search has been suspended.'

'What happened?'

'We don't know anything other than there were two on board and they've been injured. We don't even know how badly. Reg Underwood just called it in on his radio. He saw the crash and we need you at the scene.'

Adele Stokes and Steve Liebelt were instantly attracted to one another when they met in 1979. He was a tough but gentle country cop and she a fiesty city girl looking for adventure.

The Liebelts made the picture perfect family as they began their new lives at Dunmarra.

The Liebelt kids, big and raw-boned like their parents, scooped the pool at the annual sports carnival each year.

Greg and Clinton were as close as brothers could be in a neighbourhood where playmates were hundreds of kilometres away.

Clinton on his motorbike. The boys were allowed to ride on a track behind the roadhouse, but never across the other side of the Stuart Highway.

Clinton, pictured at a rodeo a few weeks before his disappearance, was the epitome of an outback boy.

Clinton's favourite toy was his teddy bear, Victor. Clinton also lined his room with toy trolls to watch over him—a cowboy, pilot, soldier and even a troll wearing a backpack. They matched the people who would search for him—stockmen, pilots, army and townspeople.

The Liebelt boys and their maternal grandfather, Vic Stokes, could float a raft in the dam across the road during the early, wet months of the year. By October it would be a cracked pan of dust.

Margie was horrified. Here she was, alone and just managing to cope with one crisis, and suddenly there was a full-scale medical emergency that would normally need a team of medics. It was a bloody nightmare. She ran to the ambulance parked near the makeshift clinic, grabbing supplies she might need, including neck braces. There could be spinal injuries to deal with out there.

Adele had not moved. She watched silently as Margie was led aboard the rescue helicopter which rose in a red blizzard and made its way to the north-west. A few minutes before it had been waiting to take her and Margie to Clinton; now it was gone. Her hopes had been shattered once more.

※ ※ ※

John Dyer and Sam Borg had flown further west after discovering Clinton's jeans. They landed a few times to check fence lines for footprints but it was a hit-and-miss affair. The scrub was too dense and they didn't have the finite skills of the trackers. The light was getting low and so was their fuel level; it was time to return to Dunmarra.

The accident happened as they swept down the northern boundary of the paddock, alongside the Buchanan Highway. John Dyer would remember it in fractions of seconds as Sam yelled out a sudden warning—'My rudder pedal is jammed. We're going in.' A spent shotgun cartridge, left after a brumby cull a few days earlier, had rolled into the joystick control panel.

The machine, now out of control, began spinning madly just 20 metres above the ground. It somehow missed four large trees as it crashed into a clearing just off the side of the road. A few metres either way and they would have been torn apart. Instead, the machine had landed upright, crushing the landing skids and flattening the seats. Above them, Reg Underwood had seen the drama unfold. He had been chatting with Sam seconds earlier as they crossed over the same search area, and heard his urgent cry over the radio. He watched in horror as the chopper spun into the clearing and settled in a sickening cloud of dust, to breathe a sigh of relief as the two men emerged from the wreckage. Dazed and shocked, John Dyer's first instinct was to get out as fast as he could, struggling with the safety harness and crawling out of the open door beneath the rotors, which were still spinning dangerously. He tried to stand but couldn't because he'd broken his collarbone in three places and most of the ribs down his left side. Sam Borg, who had injured his back, crawled clear and managed to turn off the rotors.

The accident could not have come at a worse time—a dramatic turn of events that killed the momentum created by the day's discoveries and switched attention to a rescue of a very different kind. Margie McLean, on the scene within 20 minutes, assessed the situation quickly. Sam had what looked to be a spinal injury and needed to be stabilised quickly. He was loaded onto a stretcher by other volunteers who had dashed to the scene while Margie tended to John. He was in agony, barely able to breathe through the pain of his broken bones. She gave him morphine to deaden the pain and because he was unable to lie down, squatted on the floor of the helicopter so he could lean over her knees in some sort of comfort while they flew to Daly Waters to wait for the medi-vac helicopter from Katherine. After more delay caused by the diversion of the medi-vac to another accident, the decision was made to fly the injured men directly to Katherine. They eventually landed just before midnight in the gardens of Katherine Hospital where the men would recuperate for two weeks.

For all the disruption, Margie's sudden diversion to Katherine was a blessing in disguise. For the first time in three days she was able to get a couple of hours' sleep. She also picked up more supplies of rehydration salts, bandages and dressings. When the helicopter picked her up at 4 a.m. it was still dark, and she sat alone in the back of the machine as it sped back to Dunmarra to begin a new day in the traumatic hunt.

19
They could do nothing but pray

A decade chasing cattle across the plains and woodlands of the Northern Territory had taught Mark Robins a lot about how best to see the world from the cockpit of a Robinson R-22 helicopter. Too high and you got a great view but couldn't actually distinguish much detail. Too low and you might as well be on the back of a horse. The aerial hunt for Clinton Liebelt was not dissimilar to mustering cattle, only this time the target was smaller and may not even be moving. And the stakes were also much, much higher. Back and forth he had flown over the past two days, crossing and re-crossing the same areas as he checked and re-checked the wild yellow grasslands and woolly tree groves that stretched out to the west.

As he began Tuesday, his third day in the shrill blue skies above Dunmarra, Mark was confident he had missed nothing and was beginning to think that Clinton, or more likely his body, was somewhere outside the main search area. It was not that he disagreed with the manner in which the search was being conducted, or where it was focused, but you could not help wondering why, with so many resources at their disposal, he hadn't been found. Mark had flown 12 hours on Sunday and 13 hours on Monday. Today he would do another 13, beginning at 5.45 a.m. as the sun danced across the tree tops and ending around 7.30 p.m. as it finally dropped below the horizon. The concentration was taxing, broken only by the trips back to refuel or the occasional landing to drop off searchers or food and water supplies. It made his 8- to 10-hour days during the mustering season seem like a holiday.

The morning had begun with a breakthrough of a professional kind. Manoeuvring the helicopters across the complex grid patterns was only part of the search task. The pilots' skills would be wasted without another experienced eye alongside to watch below for signs of life or, possibly, death. Mark and his fellow pilots, Steve Stanley and Sam Borg, had requested the help of three stock inspectors to join them as spotters and Fred Days, Peter Flannigan and Greg Scott had arrived overnight.

The first task of the day was to find and retrieve an army officer and his sniffer dog, dropped late the previous day into the area where Clinton's jeans had been found. In the rush to rescue John Dyer and Sam Borg the pair had unintentionally been left in the bush overnight, but the mistake was about to pay unexpected dividends. Just after 6 a.m., as they waited to be picked up, the dog stumbled onto Clinton's boots—one carefully placed behind the other—500 metres north-west of his jeans. The find was an enormous boost to the morale of the line searchers, who now numbered over 200, as they finished breakfast and prepared to travel out into the bush for the third day. The crash of the helicopter the previous night had been a shattering blow, brushing aside the excitement about the jeans. The focus of the ground search had now been moved well beyond the gas pipeline, with three separate teams working an area of 20 square kilometres between the Buchanan Highway and Kings Pond.

Alice Springs police superintendent Mick Van Heythuysen was fielding most of the media calls now, to help take the pressure off Col Hardman. Under normal circumstances a field commander might do one interview each day—if he felt like it—but Hardman could not escape media attention as he walked in and out of the roadhouse during the day. It was yet another distraction in a search that was changing by the hour as tantalising clues were found and had to be followed up. There were now at least half a dozen different sets of tracks across several kilometres being assessed as well as the clothing.

On Monday Van Heythuysen had told a reporter from the Alice Springs-based *Centralian Advocate* that finding the jeans proved that Clinton was alive in the area on Sunday night. But there were mixed messages in his assessment: 'It's good we're back on his tracks. The area had been searched pretty well on Sunday so he may have gone through again on Sunday night. But it looks like he's heading into a dry creek area and 48 hours without water for a kid is not good.'

There was still a chance of finding him alive, he'd offered: 'We haven't found his helmet or boots yet but we know by his tracks that he's now barefoot. I don't know if he could hear the helicopters and searchers during the day—we don't know what state he's in. He could be delirious and probably dehydrated. It's hard to say for a fellow his age.'

The twin finds of the jeans late on Monday and boots on Tuesday morning gave a much more serious picture of the boy's condition. Not only was he shedding clothes as the effects of dehydration set in, but his tracks now showed he was beginning to wander in wide circles. The boots were found more than a kilometre west of the set of footprints at Kings Pond, indicating that he had wandered back to the pond after taking off his boots. It was difficult to guess where he might have headed next.

* * *

Noely Campbell was convinced that Clinton was much further west than police were allowing them to search. The Yarralyn elder had said as much in his understated manner from the time he saw the boy's boot prints fleeing the darkening skies on Sunday afternoon. Pointing west across the tree tops, he told Rob Teague: 'He's gone boss, he's out there.'

In the days since nothing had dissuaded either of them that the main search area was wrong. Rob watched in a growing amazement as the tracker worked his magic through the brutal terrain. At times Noely would stand still for what seemed like an hour, slowly casting his eyes across the landscape in front of him, studying minute details just as an editor studies frames from a piece of cinematic film. The signs of Clinton's passing were there, however faint, revealed in a tiny stone flipped from its crevice, blades of grass bent the wrong way or a twig rolled by a foot so its surface was not as weathered as others around it. The clothes and footprints all pointed in the same direction. The tracks were getting older by the day but Col Hardman still refused to let his men move out of the main search area and test Rob and Noely's theory, at least not without an army or police escort. What the hell was going on? Rob understood why Hardman had to keep a tight rein on the overall search team. If everyone went off and did what they liked it could cause more problems than it solved. But Rob and his team lived in the bush for weeks at a time; it was their life, not some weekend jaunt.

The issue came to a head at a team leaders' meeting, held each evening after Hardman's general briefing of the main body of searchers. Rob Teague went as the nominated head of the stockmen who continued to gather from surrounding stations. Barry Grove went with him. These were informal meetings, held behind closed doors to allow people to vent their observations and feelings without fear of affecting the morale of the hundreds outside. Strategy was the main topic of conversation; a debriefing of the day's events and a discussion about how best to use resources tomorrow. Rob had raised his concerns every night but Hardman had held firm. He wanted everyone together. Their best information was that the boy could not travel beyond the five-kilometre radius around the clothes. Yes, it was true that the grid searches were going over the same ground from day to day—east-west one day and north-south the next—but it was necessary to ensure they missed nothing.

Rob Teague had had enough. He was already under pressure from his boss at Newcastle Waters to pull the team out and get back to the stock camp and the muster. It was not just the physical toll on men and horses but the mental anguish, which had already reduced many of them to tearful wrecks at night. But they couldn't leave, none of them, not until they had finished what they came to do. He stood to leave: 'This is utter crap. All we want to do is follow our instincts and look further out. It won't interfere with your grid searches. We've got nothing to lose because there is nothing to find. I don't care what you say; I'm taking my blokes out there tomorrow.'

Hardman knew he had to concede some ground, but insisted that the ringers had to maintain radio contact and gave them map references so the search area could be followed. It was hard enough keeping so many tired people working together. The last thing he needed was a rebellion from some of the searchers he needed the most.

❋ ❋ ❋

Richard Sallis knew a lot about running country pubs. He had owned the Katherine Motel-Hotel for more than two decades before leasing the business and taking a job as a travelling promotions man for a Queensland brewery. It suited the character of the jovial 50-year-old who could boast that he'd enjoyed a cold beer in every roadhouse, motel and pub between Ayers Rock and the West Australian tourist Mecca of Broome. Steve Liebelt at Dunmarra was one of his favourite publicans.

News of the search for Clinton had swept through the Katherine community quickly as police mounted radio appeals for volunteers to help with the ground search. The response was immediate but it became overwhelming when television coverage on the Sunday night news bulletins showed the gravity of the situation. It seemed everyone wanted to help, Richard Sallis among them.

That night he rang the police to volunteer, not as part of the search team but to help in running the roadhouse. Richard questioned his own fitness levels in the bush and didn't want to be a hindrance, but believed his experience running a motel could be invaluable and give the Liebelts one less thing to worry about. The police were not convinced. If he was no use on a search team then he should stay away from the place, they told him.

Richard hung up, annoyed at the response. He doubted the police really understood the logistical problems the roadhouse staff would face with hundreds of people involved in the search. In a moment of belligerence, he packed his swag in the back of his station wagon and drove to Dunmarra anyway. The decision proved a godsend. Richard ran into Andy McLay as soon as he arrived, who told him there was an immediate problem of getting enough food and supplies to Dunmarra to keep the volunteers fed and as comfortable as possible.

'I'll fix it. Here's my fax number. I'll head back to Katherine and by the time I get back have a list ready to tell me what you need and where to pick it up. I'll have the stuff back here by tonight.'

Richard made two trips with his wagon filled with supplies, much of it donated by local businesses who rushed to support the search, before the gearbox burned out. By Tuesday a mini-town had sprung up and Richard switched to a five-tonne refrigerated truck to make the trip. It was a 13-hour day by the time he loaded up in the morning, made the journey, unloaded and returned to Katherine. By the end of the search he would have driven over 6000 kilometres.

※ ※ ※

Andy McLay had settled into his familiar role as the roadhouse troubleshooter, quietly ensuring the generators were coping with the extra demand and that fuel supplies were adequate to keep the fleet of vehicles now parked along the highway running. No-one bothered with the till because the cost of the operation was irrelevant.

During the day Andy helped keep an eye on Adele, watching from what he considered a respectful distance, as Vic and Pat Stokes arrived, followed a few days later by Steve's parents, Dave and Mary Liebelt, who had driven up from Adelaide. He saw her spirits lift when news broke of some small discovery and plummet again when nothing else happened. He watched her stoicism in front of others and witnessed some of the moments when the veneer of control cracked and she collapsed in a torrent of screams and tears. In the evenings Andy would seek out Steve, maybe have a beer while he gave him a quiet update on how the roadhouse and its staff were coping. He wanted Steve to feel that this burden had been lifted, but he also wanted an excuse to be near his friend.

Andy also got busy calling Steve's footy mates from his Alice Springs days. If ever there was a time that mates should stick together it was now, and he wasn't disappointed. By Tuesday night there were five of them squashed into his tiny motel unit. Aiden Burke, Rodney Mclean, Jerry Ebert, Bruce Deans and George Sabbadin had drove up together on Monday after realising that the early hopes of finding Clinton quickly had been dashed, packing little more than a footy bag each with water bottles and a few clothes. The next day they were joined by another former team-mate, Moose Pickford, who drove down from Darwin. After spending the first night in the open they welcomed the air-conditioning in Andy's unit, where they congregated each evening, trading jibes in a banter designed to defuse their growing anxieties.

※ ※ ※

Steve Liebelt was asleep when Trevor Green finally reached Dunmarra in the early hours of Tuesday morning after the long drive from Darwin. One of the few people awake was Adele, who was pacing aimlessly up and down the driveway as if waiting for Clinton to emerge from the trees on the other side of the highway. The pair just hugged as they met; nothing needed to be said.

Trevor's emotions were as much relief as anything else. Sunday and Monday had been an infuriating two days as he fought with senior officers for permission to go to Dunmarra. They believed his presence would only complicate and perhaps interfere with the command structure of the operation. Monday morning's briefing of senior operational command officers had turned into a heated affair behind closed doors, the conversation dominated by discussion of the search and the appointment of Col Hardman to take over the command of possibly the largest manhunt ever seen in the Territory.

That morning Trevor again requested permission to take leave and join the search and again was told to stay out of it. They had the best team available to handle the search and believed he would only hinder the ability of Col Hardman to do his job. They couldn't see that all Trevor wanted to do was take off his policeman's hat and help his mate. Deep down he felt it was going to be a disaster. All his experience told him that Clinton's chances of survival after two days in the bush were probably less than five per cent. He also knew that the search would attract enormous numbers of people. Trevor thought he might be able to insulate his mate from the day-to-day drama; to keep him occupied away from the main search where the well-meaning but less capable actions of volunteers could become frustrating.

Commissioner Mick Palmer finally intervened and at 5 p.m. on Monday Trevor left Darwin with another task force officer, Dennis Fields, on the seven-hour drive south.

※ ※ ※

A few hours after an anxious Trevor Green drove out of Darwin, a six-tonne truck carrying a mobile home rumbled into Dunmarra, squeezing its way into a space at the front corner of the caravan park. Aboard the strange vehicle were Pastor Mike Ellemor and his wife Evelyn, patrol padres of the Uniting Church who travelled the highways and back blocks of Australia's top end, part of the church's frontier services unit. Aged in their early fifties, and with four adult children back home in Victoria, the couple had been on the road in the Territory for two years, living in the truck (nicknamed the *Padre's Palace*) as they covered a diocese which spread from the western edge of the Gulf of Carpentaria down to the Barkly Tableland. For Mike, an ordained priest for almost two decades, the posting was a way of revisiting his own childhood; the son of a Uniting Church missionary, he had spent the first 15 years of his life in and around Arnhem Land.

Patrols usually lasted two weeks, governed mainly by the amount of fuel and food they could carry in their truck. The Ellemors had been shopping in Katherine on Monday morning, stocking up for a planned patrol to the south-west near Victoria River Downs, when they heard about the search. What better calling could there be than providing a spiritual shoulder for the grieving family and their friends? Besides, they knew Steve and Adele from previous patrols down the Stuart Highway.

Tom Williams, the Anglican priest from Tennant Creek, arrived the day before the Ellemors. They would provide a vast contrast in styles, the earnest enthusiasm of the committed Ellemors, priestly in their manner and attire, against the earthy, understated wit of the stocky, graying Anglican priest dressed mostly in army fatigues. Tom Williams had always lived by the advice of the legendary Anglican bishop of the north-west, Howell Witt, who told him that to run a ministry in the outback you needed the three Gs—'grace, grit and gumption'. Within minutes of arriving Tom would be calling on that creed as he sat and comforted Adele on a rainwater tank at the back of the roadhouse. They could do nothing but pray.

Like the Ellemors, Tom Williams was disturbed by the crisis as much because he was a father of five children as he was by being a priest. His long career in the church had taken him from the Western Australian wheatfields and the orchards of the Riverina to the tough mining towns of northern Australia. He had served with the church's volunteer arm, the Bush Church Aid Society, and been a chaplain with the Australian Defence Forces for almost seven years before retiring with the rank of major to take up the position at Tennant Creek. Though he knew the area reasonably well because of his travels over the years, Tom had only been in the town for a week when Clinton went missing.

By midday on Tuesday the number of medical and counselling staff had grown even more. Margie McLean and the Liebelt family doctor, David Brooks, who had been at Dunmarra since the search began, were joined by four social workers from Family Youth and Children's Services in Katherine, and police and emergency services peer support officers from Darwin. Two psychologists would later arrive from Alice Springs and the medical team would include another two nurses as the days went by. It was time to establish a coordinated team approach to ensure they did not end up providing mixed messages to searchers and search operations staff, who were already under obvious stress. They decided that individual daily debriefings should be a priority. Tom Williams would be responsible for military personnel, and the police and emergency services peer support officers would deal with their own colleagues. Mike Ellemor would look after Clinton's immediate family and Evelyn the roadhouse staff. Mike, Tom and the social workers would also move among the searchers as they returned at lunchtime or in the evenings, encouraging them to talk about the day's events and how they felt. A daily group briefing should also be held to let everyone know what was going on, how the search was being conducted and what progress was being made. Col Harding agreed. It would be held each evening after dinner, not only to discuss the day's events but to raise issues such as the post-trauma symptoms searchers might experience from day to day, or even months afterwards.

Then there was the Dunmarra Search Chapel—a canvas tent provided by the NTES pitched in the front corner of the caravan park behind the Ellemors' truck. With a makeshift altar decorated with flowers it held a dozen chairs set in clipped rows and accommodated a small but ever-changing congregation which attended the nightly prayer services advertised on leaflets hammered out on the word processor and printer Mike kept in the truck. A steady stream of searchers—police, army, station people and townsfolk—also found their way to the tent throughout the days and nights as people sought a quiet corner to pray. In a world of tough men and women where tears normally fell as rarely as winter rain it was a brave soul who ventured into a group prayer meeting, Mike thought.

The Liebelts were catered for separately. Mike or Tom conducted small private services two or even three times a day, mostly while the search teams were away from the roadhouse or after they had returned in the evenings. There was nothing formal about these services; more discussions of feelings, hopes and fears. As more and more of Clinton's relatives arrived from all over Australia—grandparents, uncles and aunts—these meetings grew in size and breadth of emotion.

❊ ❊ ❊

The response to Clinton's disappearance was not limited to the white community. When Margie McLean told the Aboriginal staff at the Elliott clinic about the search, word spread quickly. A missing child was a serious matter, even if it was for just a few hours, and by Sunday afternoon tribespeople began arriving at Dunmarra. Many came to support fathers or uncles who were tracking for the police, but others came just to watch and listen. A camp grew up on the southern side of the roadhouse, its size changing daily as cars and people came and went.

They offered nothing but a quiet vigil from beneath the trees until late on Tuesday afternoon, when one of the women came to speak to Adele. She was Irene Thompson, one of the health workers from Elliott, who had hovered on the fringe of the knot of family and friends that seemed to follow Adele's every move, day and night. The women elders had sent Irene with a message—*they* had found Clinton: 'He's not really lost. He is out there and the women who look after this country, they have found him. They are just looking after him until somebody comes to get him.' Margie knew what she meant. The land west of Dunmarra was women's country, a place where the spirits of tribal women went after death. They wanted Adele to be comforted knowing that the long-dead women of the Jingili people had found Clinton and were cradling him in their arms until his rescuers came.

20
I became famese

Allen Eade had never been so tired in his life, physically or emotionally, not even during the heady days as a league footballer for Collingwood and Essendon in the mid-1980s. The combination of walking for eight or nine hours a day through sometimes impenetrable bush and enduring the rollercoaster of hope and despair was taking a terrible toll on the volunteers. Sleep was patchy at best, either from worry or the constant veil of heat which refused to lift even for a few hours during the night.

Allen was at Dunmarra because, like so many of those camped around him on the floor of the roadhouse, he was stricken by the thought of a young boy lost in such terrible country and wanted to help. But there was a more pressing reason—he was Clinton's cluster teacher. Until now Allen had not realised just how personal his professional life could become. The Dunmarra Wayside Inn was a far cry from the suburban streets of Melbourne where he grew up. After his illustrious football career ended Allen had tried his hand at a variety of jobs, including a stint as a wool broker and auctioneer, before becoming a teacher.

It was a holiday to Katherine the previous Easter to visit his older brother, Rick, which had brought Allen into contact with Dunmarra. What was supposed to be a fishing trip became a job offer at the School of the Air where Rick was already working as a cluster teacher. Two weeks later he was living in the middle of Australia given the responsibility of teaching a group of children, including the Liebelt brothers, living between Mataranka and Elliott. It was the irony of a city kid being in charge of 16 country kids that made the relationship so much closer. On-air radio lessons were more about interaction than teaching; a chat room where the radio became the link in a virtual neighbourhood.

Allen tried to think back to the night he heard Clinton was missing. It was Sunday, the day after the disappearance, but it seemed so long ago. He was home having dinner with his girlfriend Bronwyn Bisley, another Katherine School of the Air teacher, when the phone rang. It was Adele Liebelt: 'I'm sorry but we won't be on air tomorrow. Clinton's gone missing and we have to search for him. I just thought you should know.'

Allen could tell by the strain in her voice that Adele was only just maintaining her composure. His decision was spontaneous: 'Okay. Look, I'm coming down there. I'll be there later tonight.'

Clinton was his pupil and he felt some responsibility. He telephoned school principal Sandi Mccue, who approved the leave, and was gone within two hours; swag and clothes tossed in the back of his station wagon.

In the first few days of the search spirits had lifted as news came in of the discovery of Clinton's jeans, boots, even a blue sock. The chatter that had dissipated in the oppressive conditions would begin again as the details of the find and what it might mean were passed down the line. They wanted to believe they were getting closer to him; that the trail was still fresh and their quarry was still alive. The pace would quicken slightly as the men and women moved forward, ears tuned to the nearest two-way radio in expectation of a shout of joy.

Even when hope began to fade the enthusiasm never wavered. When the helicopter carrying John Dyer and Sam Borg crashed on Monday afternoon, the call went out for volunteers to be dropped into the bush by helicopter, near where Clinton's jeans had been found just before the accident, and make one last effort for the day. Thirty men, including Allen Eade, stepped forward. They had already spent an exhausting day but were now offering to spend another hour searching and then jog almost six kilometres in fading light back to the Buchanan Highway.

But hope could not last. By mid week the mood was changing on the search lines, with expectant enthusiasm replaced by determined resignation. No-one said that Clinton was now almost certainly dead—the words were never uttered—but team members instinctively moved closer together on the line as they moved through the bush each morning; everyone knew they had to check more thoroughly because they were now looking not for a distraught child, but a body.

Some began to question how the search was being handled, and whether they had either missed the boy or he was beyond the tight search site which had been established around the jeans—the five-kilometre radius senior police believed would be the limit of Clinton's endurance. On Wednesday, when the radios crackled to life late in the morning to announce that more footprints had been found, the response was almost apathetic, as if they were sick of being tricked into believing there was hope by some sort of mirage. It would be easy to give up and go home, but no-one did.

Allen was also worried about Greg Liebelt. The attention all week had been focused on Clinton's desperate plight, but his older brother was also in the midst of a crisis, one which would almost certainly affect the rest of his life. The psychological trauma of a 10-year-old struggling to cope with the search for his brother was clear to everyone, manifested in a brash young kid showing off to get attention. Greg was not jealous of Clinton but drowning in the sea of despair around him; a world he could not understand and one in which he could not participate. There were also a number of other children who'd arrived earlier in the week and were now running amuck around the roadhouse while their parents were occupied with the search.

Allen raised his worries with Sandi Mccue when he made his nightly telephone call to update the school so that Clinton's classmates could feel part of the effort. Sandi was adamant that he should set up school in the classroom at the back of the roadhouse to bring some sense of normality back into the life of the children unavoidably caught up in the nightmare. She would arrange for the Department to send a couple of guidance counsellors to help. As much as Allen hated the thought of removing himself from the search team he knew that Sandi was right. One less person on the line would make little difference, but a teacher in the classroom would help the children and mean one less thing for Adele and Steve to worry about. Adele breathed a sigh of relief when told of the plan. With the best will in the world she couldn't concentrate on anything but Clinton, and Greg needed something to take his attention off the terrible events around him.

* * *

Debbie Bruce was scared; not frightened for her safety but shocked by her own naivety. She had walked less than 10 metres into the bush from the roadside where the bus had dropped the volunteers and stopped to look back. She could see nothing to tell her where she had just come from or where the searchers either side of her were standing. The bullwaddy in front of her looked impossible to get through; its angry branches spiked as if daring her to try and pass without getting on her hands and knees to crawl through the tangle. In that moment, as she forced aside the matted cobwebs and resisted the stabbing branches, Debbie finally understood the gravity of Clinton's situation.

She had left the roadhouse for the first time that Wednesday morning borrowing a long-sleeved cotton shirt from Adele because her own hastily prepared wardrobe was hopelessly inadequate, and jumping on one of the 5 a.m. buses with 200 other ground search volunteers. As much as it hurt her to leave Adele for the day, she had to get away from the roadhouse; to get out there in the scrub with the rest of the volunteers and do something, anything to help find Clinton. It had been three days and she was going crazy waiting for something to happen. It went against her nature to sit around reading magazines while there was work to be done, reduced to watching the faces of the task force commanders as radio calls came in from the field in the hope there would be good news.

Debbie was there for Adele, of course, but now Adele had her mother and her family to watch over her. Adele didn't want to search. She wanted to stay at the roadhouse, to be there for Clinton when they brought him home. It was her way of staying positive; never letting go of the belief that they would find him and everything would be okay. Debbie clung to the same hope, no matter what the talk was around the roadhouse each night.

As she regained her feet the other side of the bullwaddy and faced a field of lancewood, Debbie realised for the first time what Adele meant when she'd phoned in a panic on that first night and said Clinton was *lost*. She had left Alice Springs with a small bag packed with shorts and a couple of t-shirts, expecting the crisis would be over by the time she arrived or he would be found within a day or so, tired and sunburned but otherwise okay.

But this was not the desert bush that Debbie was used to around Alice Springs, where the heat was dry, the plants edible and you could climb a ridge top to judge where you were going or be seen by rescuers. Clinton might have stood a chance in that country, but not here. This was a bloody awful jungle—flat, featureless country filled with tangled trees that offered nothing but an obstacle course that went nowhere but further into hell. She had left the roadhouse a few hours ago convinced that Clinton was still alive. Now she was convinced he was dead.

Debbie understood now why the search teams came back exhausted and demoralised every night; why everyone said they felt useless. She had helped Adele invent scenarios about how her younger son was still alive and waiting to be rescued, refusing to accept even the remotest possibility that the search wouldn't be successful. They had found fun in the midst of the sadness, giggling like schoolgirls as they spied on the handsome young task force officers getting changed in the roadhouse office, laughing at the way the soldiers polished their boots each night, as if someone was going to notice, or care, the next day when they set off before anyone else to search another patch of desolate scrub.

But now, after seeing the truth herself, Debbie didn't want to feed her friend any more false hopes. She understood why grown men and women suddenly burst into tears; hardened bush people like Joan Davey, who she'd met back in the Kulgera days when she and her husband, Luke, were contracted by cattle stations to track and catch wild horses. Brumby runners, they were called. Joan and Luke's relationship with Steve and Adele was little more than a social one, but Joan had stayed close friends with Debbie since. As soon as she heard about Clinton's disappearance she insisted on joining the search.

The hardest part of the search for Joan was not the physical effort in the bush each day—something she was used to after living in bush camps for years—but arriving back at the roadhouse each evening and seeing Adele and her mother waiting, expectantly, in the driveway to greet and thank them individually for the efforts she knew had failed to find her son. It was heart-rending.

Joan had cracked the previous night. She didn't feel like eating and just wanted to be alone with the grief that threatened to overwhelm her. She walked out the back, leaned on the back of her four-wheel-drive and began to sob uncontrollably. She didn't want to stop, not even when one of the other searchers found her. He was a total stranger but in that moment they were comrades in an experience they wouldn't wish on their worst enemy. They embraced and cried together.

* * *

Adele sat alone in Clinton's room. She wanted to be as close as possible to her younger son. The boys had slept together all their lives until a couple of months ago, when Greg decided he wanted his own space. Clinton hated the idea. The two things he feared more than anything else were the dark and being alone; having a room to himself meant he had to endure both every night. As she sat on the bed Adele cast her eyes around a space she usually regarded only as a constant mess. Little things now took on a different meaning, like the contents of a time capsule Clinton had made out of an old coffee jar a few months before for a school project. It had been buried in the backyard but Greg had somehow recovered it when his brother went missing. Adele unscrewed the lid and gently removed the odd collection of artefacts. There was a blurred photograph of Clinton blowing out the candles on his eighth birthday cake six months before, and a timeline of a typical day in his life. '7.15: I woke up and got dressed. I had Weet-Bix for breakfast. 8am: Radio lesson, school work,' it began. Adele managed a slight smile. Clinton was hopeless in the morning, mainly because he was so difficult to get to bed at night. '10am: Morning tea. 10.30: School. 12.00: Lunchtime. 1pm: Back to school. 3pm: Play in the yard. 6pm: Tea time.' And that's where it ended; no mention of bed time, of course.

Also rolled up in the jar were two letters, complete with the spelling mistakes of an eight-year-old: 'In July 1993 I was 141cm tall, I weigh 35kg my shoe size is 5 and a half. I like playing with my Nintendo. My favourite game is Kidicisss. I like to watch Chipmunks. My favirit food is Jelly and lettece and backed beens and vegetables.'

The second letter underlined the imagination of a child: 'One day I was climbing a mountain and I sliped and fell into a cave. I picked up a rock and there was a toolbox. There was all kind of jewelry in the box. I looked underneath the box and it said Black Beard. I took the box to a collector and he gave me millions of dollars. I became famese.'

Then the ugly little trolls dotted around the room drew her attention. Clinton had set them up, bought with pocket money one day and positioned to watch over him as he slept. There was a cowboy, a pilot, a soldier and even a troll wearing a backpack. They matched the people now out there hunting for him—the ringers, helicopter pilots, army and police and the townspeople. Did he have a premonition? Was it an omen?

Adele's thoughts drifted to death. It was a distant, unfamiliar notion to her. She couldn't remember the death of anyone close enough to have touched her deeply. Not in her whole sheltered life. The only death she had ever known, as a child, was that of her great grandmother, Ester Louise Endersby, who had emigrated with Adele's grandmother when she was 88. She was moved into a nursing home within months because of her frailty, but the family would visit several times a week. On weekends the old lady was often strapped into the car and taken on the weekly trip to the rubbish tip. It seemed ridiculous now, looking back on it, but Ester loved the outing and insisted on buying ice-creams for the kids on the return journey. When she died quietly one day Adele and the other children weren't allowed to go to the funeral. They went to school instead and were taken later that day to the grave to see the flowers their pocket money had bought. Adele thought they were pretty, not sad. For years she would visit the grave and take a bouquet of blue and white flowers—her great-grandmother's favourite colours. Her passing seemed a matter of course rather than a moment to grieve.

This was different. This was real, and cruel. There was no use ignoring the truth any more, by pretending there was still a chance her little boy was still alive out there. He was dead; she knew it in her heart. No-one could survive in that heat—52 degrees on the ground, police had told her. She just hoped the end was kind—in his sleep maybe and that he was at peace. It was all she could ask.

Sleep was what she wanted too. Sleep, even for a few hours, so she didn't have to face the people out there. She didn't want to talk to them anymore; she didn't want to listen to their theories and their attempts to comfort her. It didn't matter. Clint was dead. The days just rolled on into one another. She felt helpless and utterly useless.

Adele asked Dr Brooks to help her sleep but Greg overheard her and thought she was being put down like the dog they had to kill last year. The poor kid; how could she expect him to hold it together when the adults were struggling? When she'd finally convinced Greg that she was just going to sleep for a few hours, she took her mother aside and gave her a bag packed with Clint's clothing, including his teddy bear Victor. It would give him some sense of security when they found him.

'Mum, I have to sleep now,' she told Patricia Stokes. 'If they find him please go to him. Make him feel safe until I can get there.'

Patricia wept, promising to carry out her wishes even though she had no intention of leaving her daughter's side.

21
I'll never stop searching

The media coverage kept pace with the most optimistic assessments of those on the ground—that there was still hope, albeit slim, of finding Clinton alive. As the days passed and the search team continued to swell, national newspapers and television also picked up on the story. It even captured attention in Europe and North America, where the imagined dangers of the outback only added to its distant romance. As much as the story centred on the search for a lost boy its appeal lay in the notion that hundreds of people were camping by the side of a lonely desert highway each night, each day searching for a boy most of them didn't even know. What was driving this overwhelming display of community spirit, and how long could it last?

The journalists and their editors wanted to believe there was still a chance of finding Clinton alive, as did the thousands who followed the search at a distance and hoped it would result in another miracle, like that of Queenslander James Scott who'd survived for 43 days in the Himalayas the year before on nothing but ice and chocolate bars. The trouble was that Clinton had neither. From Col Hardman and Mick Van Heythuysen's perspective, there was no sense in shattering the hopes and enthusiasm of hundreds of volunteers by declaring that Clinton was dead, even if they believed it themselves. They spoke to reporters each evening in terms of Clinton's survival chances and the search team's progress as they followed his trail of clothing in ever-widening circles to the west.

But the headline and story across the front page of the *Northern Territory News* on Thursday morning—'Hopes fading for little lost Clinton'—reluctantly carried the message that their goal now was to bring home his remains. It was time to prepare the public for the awful truth.

Mick Van Heythuysen pulled no punches: 'In reality, hope virtually has petered out. I think it has dawned on everyone that there's not much chance of him surviving. But everyone wants to finalise the situation by at least finding his body. The response to this has been incredible. The support is overwhelming. I think the whole situation has touched everyone's heart, but it's a huge operation and we have to be careful not to endanger any searchers.'

Despite the sense they were clinging to a miracle, there was no decision yet to scale down the operation: 'The search is continuing at full pace, with 50-man line searches through the area where his jeans and boots were found. We have some of the best trackers here but the ground is very difficult. A few tracks are found in dusty areas and then nothing more for a kilometre or so.'

What was left unsaid was that the search parties had been following a trail of death for the past few days. Rather than raising spirits, the discovery of clothing was a signpost for concern. From the moment John Dyer spotted Clinton's jeans on Monday he knew that the boy was dying, shedding his clothes as he succumbed to the ravages of dehydration.

In truth, Clinton had begun to lose his battle with the elements when fear, or perhaps naive bravado, caused him to leave his motorbike. Like the dying madness of teenagers James Annetts and Simon Amos seven years before, Clinton ended up walking in circles as his body overheated and his mind became disoriented. The experts call this desert delirium and paradoxic undressing, because the discarded clothing would help rather than hinder survival.

There were more signposts that morning as line searches were set up on either side of the track bulldozed through to Kings Pond the day before. Mounted police retraced a search area between Dunmarra and the gas pipeline, then turned south and followed the track to the abandoned No. 8 Bore in case Clinton had back-tracked behind the main search lines. A separate group of 50 army personnel were dropped into the bush south of where the clothing had been found. Helicopters continued overhead.

Mark Robins was working independently now. He took a spotter at first light, making giant sweeps as far as the western fenceline of the paddock which lay 25 kilometres from Dunmarra, then following it 15 kilometres to the southern boundary. He flew back to Dunmarra for a three-hour rest before rejoining the main aerial search team and flying intensive east-west lines from Kings Pond to the south, through what the command centre had assessed was the most probable area in which they would find what most believed would be a body rather than a child.

At 7.45 a.m. Clinton's second sock was found a few metres from the first. It did nothing but emphasise how difficult conditions were. At 11 a.m. Bob Christianson spotted Clinton's goggles just over a kilometre south-west of the boots, which confirmed he was still forging west, albeit in wide arcs. Trackers were brought in immediately but the trail was getting cold. There were no strobe lights or water set out that night, and the medi-vac helicopter had gone back to Katherine.

The only other 'find' that day was the runaway horse, Phoenix. The chopper pilots had seen the horse on the second day of the search, wandering unharmed in the north-west corner of the paddock but no-one was in a hurry to recover the animal whose disappearance had sparked the tragic sequence of events. Dave Langan was in the middle of a line search when he heard the news that his horse had been recaptured. He wished it was dead.

* * *

There was an incident that kept repeating itself inside Peter Kerr's head; the day he and Steve were driving back from a trip to Katherine with the kids in the back seat. It was a few months back, on one of the frequent trips he made up from Alice. All the kids were quiet except Clinton, who was pestering his father about being allowed to enter a mini-marathon. He was going on and on, as only Clinton could, until finally Steve stopped the car at the Buchanan Highway turn-off, eight kilometres from Dunmarra, and offered his son a simple challenge: 'Reckon you can run a marathon? Okay, if you can run all the way to Dunmarra from here you can enter the race.'

Clinton grinned, leapt out of the car and raced off down the highway like a rabbit, then stopped barely 200 metres from where Steve and Peter sat in amusement. He trotted back and opened the car door.

'Can't run in these,' he said, tossing his shoes in the back seat. Then he was off again.

Steve shrugged. 'We'll head back to Dunmarra, wait a while and then I'll go out and get him,' he said as he drove off, checking in the rear vision mirror in case Clinton changed his mind. He didn't.

They'd got back to Dunmarra and had a cup of tea before Steve looked at his watch. 'I'll go and get Clint. He'll have had enough by now.'

As they got up, Clint came bouncing through the door on the balls of his feet, barely out of breath. 'See, I told ya, I told ya.'

Funny as it seemed at the time, the incident now made Peter weep, haunting him like a nightmare portent ignored. Clinton's enthusiasm for life, and his amazing stamina for an eight-year-old, were probably the primary causes of his predicament. He quietly questioned the wisdom of the police who'd limited the search area to a five-kilometre radius around the clothes they had found three days before. They didn't think an adult, let alone a young boy, could travel any further in such horrendous conditions. Peter thought otherwise.

Peter tried to put himself in the shoes of a kid like Clinton who hated the dark, even in his own environment, who wouldn't even play outside with the other kids after sunset. The poor kid would have been terrified out there in the bush, alone. There was no way he would have sat down at night and waited until morning. He'd have run like fuck, pushing through grass over his head and smashing into every tree. In the back of his mind he'd be thinking that Dunmarra would be behind the next bush. That's probably why he didn't stop at the gas pipeline road that first night; he was running so hard he never saw it. There were so many turns he could have made that would have led him to safety, but he took the wrong one every time. It was pure fate.

Then there were the questions put to him at the roadhouse each night, from friends, family, even strangers, all searching for answers. They seemed to flock to Peter as if he would have the magical answer and that everything would still be all right. What do you say to someone like Adele's parents, standing in front of you at 10 o'clock at night pleading for a sliver of hope that their grandson—your godchild—is still alive? Do you give them false hope or do you force them to face reality? In the end he bullshitted and told them what they wanted to hear. The last thing you needed was more insecurity and emotion. Back at the roadhouse everyone was just holding together.

Peter was also running out of ideas to keep Steve occupied. He, Trevor Green, Glenn Stokes and another of Steve's close friends, policeman Mick Reid, had managed to keep Steve busy for the past four days, creating their own search area each day to ensure they stayed away from the main ground teams. They feared the repercussions of Steve being involved each day on the line search—frustrations building as the methodical coverage yielded little but heatstroke and heartache. This morning they had finally relented and sent him out on a search line for a few hours. It seemed to break the tension and Steve was happy to be taken off it again just before lunch. The only news that morning was that Clinton's goggles had been found by one of the chopper pilots; the sort of discovery that would have caused excitement even a day before but was now regarded as just another mirage. They felt like the Three Musketeers, forming a protective barrier around a man who was hiding his emotions but clearly struggling as each day passed without a resolution. Peter had caught his mate the previous night crossing the highway, ready to walk into the bush by himself.

'Where are you going? It's two o'clock in the morning.'

'Fuck it, I'm going to find him.'

'Mate, you're not going to do it on your own. Come on.'

Amidst the despair there had been moments when the physical and emotional strains lifted ever so slightly. One afternoon Steve had stopped suddenly, groaned and dropped his pants. The others watched, amused, as he reached into a backpack and pulled out a white jar of what looked like moisturising cream. He stood there in the middle of the bush, legs splayed, and sighed with satisfaction as he took great dollops of the stuff with his big hands and smeared it between thighs rubbed raw from days of bush walking. Pawpaw cream, it turned out to be; donated in case-loads by someone in Katherine. It was a godsend. As Steve stood there one of the emergency services crews approached him, saw the cream and asked if he could have some. Steve nodded. The bloke wiped his finger in the cream and smeared his bottom lip which had been chafing in the sun. The others collapsed laughing as he turned up his nose at the slight odour.

But the laughter was fleeting. It was just after 3 p.m. on Thursday when the four men sat down on a bush track near the abandoned No. 8 Bore at the southern boundary of the paddock for a break. The area had been searched at least a dozen times, in the hope that Clinton had somehow backtracked behind the search lines overnight. There wasn't much to say as they ate. Conversations had dwindled to the necessary rather than any form of banter. Peter, the incessant joker, tried to fill the yawning gap by lamenting his decision to give up smoking because they could probably all do with one at the moment. The others nodded in agreement but the quip fell flat.

Steve broke the silence: 'I know he's gone but I'll never stop searching.'

* * *

The silver gums guarding the Katherine Showgrounds stood listless in the late afternoon heat, waiting for the merest breeze to wake their graceful limbs and stir the coal-black crows perched on their branches as if on a grandstand to watch the activity below. The birds' mournful calls echoed across the ground, matching the mood of the 20 or so players from the Kirby's Agents Football Club as they went through the managed paces of Thursday night training. Their hearts weren't in it tonight, not because of the heat but because it was difficult to concentrate on handball drills and kicking practice in the fading light when hope was fading even faster in the race to find young Clinton Liebelt.

The search had been the only topic of conversation in the town all week—a nightmare scenario which only served to highlight the fear and respect for the bush that only those who lived in, and loved, the outback could understand. Perhaps that was why so many people had wanted to help. There had been emergencies before which had required a community response—searches even—but nothing on this scale.

Hundreds had put their personal and professional lives on hold to drive or be taken by army bus to help a family in need. The nightly convoy would leave some time after midnight, timed to arrive by dawn when the first search parties were briefed and assigned their plot of hell. Some would spend a day in the bush, wash away the dust with a cold beer and return to the domestic sanctuary of Katherine to hug their own children. Others would phone home to say goodnight, roll out a swag and camp overnight by the side of the highway.

The conversation continued in earnest after training finished just after 7 p.m. when players and officials traditionally adjourned for team selection to the pub after which the club was named. Kirby's was the bar at the Katherine Hotel-Motel which stood on a main street remarkable for nothing visually but its width—to accommodate the road trains. The team was born here five years before from a conversation between the bar's owner, Peter Walkington, and some of his regular customers—a bunch of Elders stock agents.

The club's players and officials felt a special affinity with the Liebelt family. Not only was Steve a sponsor of the club but most of the Elders boys had got to know the family well as they travelled up and down the Stuart Highway visiting the district's cattle stations. Team selection was all but forgotten as the night drew on and the topic of conversation persisted. Craig Baird, the team's burly centre half-forward and a town copper, had been told by colleagues that there were problems down at Dunmarra. It was inevitable as time went by and the boy was still not found that patience would wear thin and tempers begin to fray. There was even word that Steve Liebelt's hospitality (nobody was paying for a drink at the bar) was being abused. Everybody was tired and at their wits' end. There was a desperate need for fresh legs.

It was decided in a moment. Nobody would ever remember who made the suggestion, but club president Wes Binks made the announcement. The team would forfeit their games on the weekend at the annual pre-season lightning carnival. They would organise a bus on Friday night and go to Dunmarra for the weekend. They would take everything they needed—food, grog, barbecues, ice and swags—so they were self-sufficient and didn't make life any more difficult for the Liebelts. There wasn't a murmur of dissent.

The police weren't so sure when told the next morning. The last thing they needed was a busload of yahooing, headstrong footballers looking for an excuse to get out of town for the weekend and get pissed. It was difficult enough controlling the people they already had in an environment becoming increasingly agitated by the lack of success. It had been two days since anything of significance was found, and the chances of finding the boy alive had all but vanished. It took the support of league officials, who had accepted the forfeiture, to finally sway search leaders to accept the offer. Peter Walkington had been on the line searches since Monday and driven back to Katherine to arrange the bus for the club. He called a final meeting on Friday evening at 5 p.m. Anyone who wanted to go must have their bags packed and be ready by 7 p.m. When it left two hours later the bus was packed.

22
The best of people

Jon Finn felt like an intruder. The *Toowoomba Chronicle* journalist had made a 2500-kilometre road trip from southern Queensland in just 32 hours to join the search, not for professional reasons but to support his mate and brother-in-law Kim Stokes, who had moved back to Toowoomba, the town where the family had spent the years that Adele treasured most from her childhood.

But in the three days Jon had been on the search team, walking from sun-up until dusk and sleeping barely two hours a night, the experience had evolved into something much more than supporting a friend. He was watching a major national and international story unfold; a nightmare that had trapped its participants, including himself, in an emotional spiderweb whose bonds could only be loosed by a resolution. Yet Jon could not cover the story because he felt it would betray the confidence of those around him who watched with threadbare tolerance the daily arrival of television and print journalists striving to capture the human drama. Jon felt the searchers' suspicion of his colleagues; the sense that the film crews were there to cover an event rather than show concern about a family in distress. He didn't disagree with them.

As a small town journalist he had grown to resent the impact of media personalities who became as big as the stories they covered. The reality was lost in the hype and, worse, it tarred the rest of them with the same brush, even the genuine reporters like himself who did their job in its purest form—to keep the public informed. But even on this scale, Jon had doubts. The local papers were doing their best but the tiny mistakes which constantly seemed to creep into their copy, like the wrong search locations, made him cringe. As the week drew to a close the stories were getting bleaker, and the interest of the world outside was waning. Jon despaired. He wanted to make a difference, and write a story from inside the search, to try to capture its spirit and perhaps stem the loss of hope which seemed to be trickling slowly into the Dunmarra dust.

As Jon struggled with the dilemma, his hand-written diary revealed the story he wanted to tell in print. Among his own torn feelings as the father of a girl the same age as Clinton Liebelt he noted the personal sacrifices of the searchers—the ringers who opted to have their wages cut rather than go home before they had found Clinton, the dying woman who told her son to stay on at Dunmarra rather than rush home to her bedside because he should stay where his help was needed most, and the young girl who came down from Katherine on a bus to spend her birthday on the search team with her parents.

He witnessed the raw emotion—saw Steve embrace his eldest son Ben to say how much he loved him before heading out for another day's search, the struggle of senior police to hold their emotions in check as they gave the latest update to the media, and Adele's nightly vigils in the roadhouse 'to keep Clint company'. There were the occasional snatches of humour, like the woman with spear grass in her undies who thought she had been bitten by a snake, and the man whose pants went missing in the wash and was warned to wear plenty of sunscreen on his bum the next day. But most of all Jon recorded the unity and spirit of the search teams, 'like a little slice of heaven even with the tragedy that clouds everything. There is no bickering or pettiness, no colour prejudice or materialistic thoughts. This is the best of people and I doubt I will see it again.'

* * *

The media attention and constant demands for interviews was draining on Adele. Getting through the disappointment of each day was hard enough without having to relive it in newspaper headlines or on television each night. She had stopped answering the phones because she was sick of pretending to be someone else. Adele now knew why Lindy Chamberlain had reacted so strangely to the barrage of media attention, she empathised with the woman who'd grieved with a stony mask and was accused of being callous because of it. Adele wanted to maintain a strong, dignified demeanour in the face of her son's disappearance but feared it could be interpreted the wrong way. It was a risk she would not take.

When Col Hardman briefed the search teams one morning about the approaching media hordes, he asked that the family's identity be kept secret. Neither Steve nor Adele was ready to talk about Clinton; at least not while the search was still going on. They wanted to remain anonymous faces in the crowd at the roadhouse, free to go about their business without the sense that a camera was following their every move, waiting for their emotions to give way in grief, anger or even laughter. Miraculously, no-one gave them away.

Adele watched one day as a television crew filming inside the roadhouse spied a young boy in one corner of the busy room and began to follow his movements. The boy noticed too, uncertain of how to handle the unwanted attention as the camera zoomed in on his impassive freckled face whenever he turned around. It was uncomfortable. He wanted to get away but the lens followed as he walked across the room. They only became more interested as he began talking to a blonde-haired woman sitting at the main table. Adele wondered why they would be interested in Danniel and his mother Lu. As they continued to film the pair walking out of the room, the answer became obvious; the crew thought they'd found Adele and Greg.

Then there was the constant stream of calls from the psychics and clairvoyants. They phoned day and night with theories and claims that did nothing but play on the hopes of desperate people and divert precious resources. The dilemma for the search leaders was that they couldn't afford to totally dismiss psychic claims, even though they all knew such leads were likely to result in a wild goose chase and be a waste of time. One woman reckoned the tail rotor of the crashed helicopter in which John Dyer and Sam Borg were injured pointed the way to Clinton sitting on a ridge somewhere five kilometres away. They found nothing, not even the promised ridge. Another sent the choppers off to find a billabong where Clinton was apparently resting, despite the fact that there wasn't a waterhole within 100 kilometres of Dunmarra.

Others had dreamed of coordinates on a map—again nothing. Adele had answered the phone to a couple of them herself. One called in the early hours of the morning while Adele was making sandwiches, insisting he had been contacted by Clinton and could prove it by nominating his favourite song.

'Okay, what is it?' Adele challenged.

There was a hesitation at the other end of the line. 'I'm a little teapot,' he finally offered. Adele hung up. Clinton was a Garth Brooks fan.

At least Adele was finding it easier to survive the nights. She didn't even attempt to sleep after dark. Instead she helped with the evening meals and then tended bar for the few men who wanted to drink. Even though the beer and rum was free there weren't many who could face more than a couple to wash away the dust. Most were ready for bed as soon as they'd eaten and washed, or had waited in the nightly queue outside to use the public phone and call their own families. After the bar shut down at 11 p.m. Adele would busy herself in the kitchen with roadhouse staff Deidre Davis, Julie Meldrum, Molly Kerby, Jannelle Evans, Wendy Rogers and Joanne Murphy. They made hundreds of rounds of sandwiches for the day ahead, filling and freezing water bottles and piling oranges into boxes; anything to keep busy and stifle the crushing thoughts of her son.

There was always someone around to talk to and pass the time. Val Brooks was helping to keep the roadhouse running for the tourists and truckies who still stopped by, as much to offer their help or run an errand as anything else. Their conversations would drift from politics to sport; anything to avoid the events outside. Inevitably though, their thoughts would return to the search. Adele's words were now devoid of most emotion; more robotic, matter-of-fact assessments or the recounting of amusing interludes such as her father's jocular offer to inspect the men's scrotums as they returned, legs chafing despite layers of pawpaw cream, from another 10 hours in the sun.

As dawn was breaking she would help feed the masses their breakfast and listen to their assessments, which always seemed to be more upbeat at the beginning of the day, before collapsing for a few hours' rest as soon as the search crews left on the buses. Sleep came quickly now, though never for more than a few hours.

It seemed to some of those watching that Adele had accepted that there was nothing else to do but wait. Adele had never been particularly spiritual but the words of the Elliott Aboriginal women had somehow struck a chord and given her a little peace. She wanted to believe in the mystic spirits out there, those long-dead Jingili tribeswomen who were protecting her Clintypops, Steve's Possum, until they could bring him home.

* * *

By Friday morning the search had officially become the biggest manhunt in Northern Territory history and one of the largest in Australia. No-one was keeping an accurate count of the human traffic through Dunmarra, but an estimated 1200 people had become involved at some stage during the week, either physically searching, working at the roadhouse to keep everyone fed and clothed or delivering supplies. Many were still wearing the same clothes they'd arrived in days earlier. Caught up in an experience, a human endeavour they could not abandon, it was as if the search had somehow become a test of their self-worth, individually and as a community.

Col Hardman was still turning people away, placing them on standby rosters to replace those who had to rest or return to the world outside Dunmarra. He also wanted to keep injuries to a minimum, and the more people out searching the greater the risk of injuries. They were facing enough injury problems already. The campsite looked like a hospital ward by late afternoon as dozens were treated each day for exhaustion and wounds. Margie McLean's motel clinic was now dealing with as many as 50 people a day as the effects of four or five days in the bush and little sleep combined to take their toll. Most needed salt tablets and a few hours' rest, or bandages for cuts, scrapes and twisted ankles, but several had been evacuated to hospital in Katherine. When Margie and two assistants brought up from Elliott weren't helping exhausted volunteers they were bandaging the blistered feet of army servicemen whose boots had proved a liability in the bush. And it was not only people who were suffering. The sniffer dogs made a pitiful sight, lying motionless on long wooden benches in the evening as worried handlers gently poured water over their coats. The heat was bad enough for them but the dust was debilitating, literally choking them as they hunted for clues on the packed earth. One dog would die before the search was finally over.

Despite the problems and frustrations and ultimately the disappointment of the unsuccessful search, neither Col Hardman nor his superiors in Darwin were ready to withdraw their resources, even when it became obvious there was virtually no chance of finding the boy alive. Dunmarra was now much more than a desperate search for life; to give up without a resolution in the face of such an overwhelming display of community spirit would have left a gaping hole not only in the morale of the search team but also the thousands who were watching from afar, holding their breath and hoping for a miracle.

Hardman told the media not to expect a miracle: 'It's only two days short of a week now and without food or water in that country and those temperatures you'd have to rate his chances as slim at best. But the searchers are still as keen as ever and they're hoping we can find him alive. In this country it's hard moving anywhere and without his boots he is not going to get far. We know he headed west since getting off his bike but then his boots, jeans, goggles and socks are all over the place. It is impossible to stay on his tracks.'

Mick Van Heythuysen said that unlike the previous clothing discoveries, finding the goggles had not raised anyone's hopes of finding him alive. Steve and Adele were facing the reality of the situation: 'They are obviously extremely distressed but I think they've acknowledged the overwhelming likelihood that they must prepare for the worst.'

23

Orange people

Mark Robins and Steve Stanley were running out of ideas. They had spent five hours on Friday morning combing an area south of where the boots had been found three days before but retrieved nothing other than a white water bottle cap. No-one even pretended that it might belong to Clinton. The excitement of finding orange peel a few days before had long since disappeared, as had any suggestion that he had taken a haversack of provisions when he left the roadhouse. The boy had been without food and water for a week, and the chances of finding anything to eat or drink in this country were all but impossible. Animal life was almost non-existent and any overnight moisture was quickly sucked dry as the sun rose.

The biggest mystery apart from Clinton's whereabouts was what had happened to his helmet. If they could spy a bottle top or an orange peel from the air, why couldn't they see a white, full-faced motorcycle helmet? Maybe he'd dropped it into a hole or it was buried in the undergrowth beneath a tree. Whatever had happened, Steve Liebelt's insistence that his son would keep the helmet with him as some sort of security seemed to be accurate. Even though he was shedding clothes, Clinton was still carrying the helmet. If they could find it, they would find the boy.

The helicopters flitted back and forth between Dunmarra and the search teams for the rest of the day, dropping supplies or evacuating searchers and checking out claims by a clairvoyant that Clinton was at a billabong in the north-west corner of the paddock. As they had expected it came to nothing but they used the excursion as an excuse to run search lines much further to the west than had been attempted before.

That evening their spotters, the stock inspectors, were sent home. Their expertise was needed elsewhere. Bob Christianson followed, his flying hours dangerously high, and Mark Robins was told he had one day left before he also had to stand down for a rest. Steve Stanley would be working by himself by Monday morning.

Nothing would be found again on Saturday but the volunteers kept coming. Stations continued to rotate their men and horses and fresh task force officers were being sent down from Darwin every second day. The Kirby's Agents footballers arrived as promised and the NTES continued to find replacements from across the Territory. On Friday night more than 100 NTES men and women—'orange people' or 'carrots' as they had become affectionately known—had left, many in tears. Steve Twentyman, a 15-year veteran with the NTES, had been the one to make the emotional decision that enough was enough after 8000 man-hours of searching over five days. His volunteers had come rushing to help in record numbers as soon as they had heard that a child was missing and now they were being told to stand down without a result, successful or not.

The next morning a busload of more than 20 fresh NTES volunteers rolled into Dunmarra from Alice Springs. Trevor Haines, who managed the southern region of the organisation, was aboard with his wife Chris. They had all been involved in search-and-rescue operations before but the crisis at Dunmarra was bigger than anything they could remember. Displaying blind faith perhaps, they arrived with the hope that the boy could still be found alive. The next evening they would leave in despair, for he was still out there.

Jon Finn had been in Katherine for the past 24 hours, taking time out to rest and to visit his brother's family. He had slept less than six hours since leaving Toowoomba and was close to breaking, physically and emotionally. Jon had finally written the story he craved, seeking Adele's approval before offering to his newspaper and the wire services an account he hoped would rekindle what he feared was flagging outside interest. Now on his way back to Dunmarra to rejoin the search, he anxiously scanned the radio stations as he drove, hoping his efforts had helped lift the story back into the hourly bulletins. There it was, third on the list at 10 a.m. He felt justified, as if the search was again alive with some sense of hope. It had been a difficult task to convey the emotion behind the scenes.

> You have to beat your way through the scrub; there are no landmarks and there is no high ground where you can get an extended view. The only thought in my mind while beating through the bush from daylight to dark is 'Where is he?' The only word to describe this country is eerie—there are no animals or birdlife—it's as though the animals won't go there for some reason. It's unbelievable to think that so many people could comb an area so thoroughly and not find this little boy. So far the searchers have found Clinton's goggles, boots, socks and trousers but not together. They have found fresh tracks on ground that has been searched previously but the tracks don't lead anywhere or come from anywhere. There are people here from all over Australia. Despite being exhausted and emotionally drained they say they won't give up until Clinton is found. The family hasn't requested help maintaining the search but they need it; this nightmare has to end.

The weekend papers had followed suit, filled with stories and features that told of the sadness and heroics of the past week. But among the tributes the message was clear that this was the last roll of the dice. The search would be scaled down over the weekend and probably abandoned early next week. Jon could sense the change in mood when he arrived back at the roadhouse. The enthusiasm was still there but the precision of the line searches was beginning to wane as the constant change in personnel took its toll on consistency. Every morning there seemed to be 20 or more new people to teach how to walk in a straight line. Tempers frayed more easily and accidents were becoming more frequent as the search moved deeper into the empty paddock and men and women grew more tired in the unyielding heat. Jon learned to dry his sweaty head under the downdraught from the rotor blades of the choppers as they took off after dropping supplies or evacuating yet more searchers who'd had enough. And the water each of them carried in plastic bottles strung at their sides by pieces of rope was so warm by midday that they longed for tea bags to make a cuppa instead.

* * *

Given the choice between flying and driving, Dave Moore would always take the latter. The Assistant Police Commissioner of the Alice Springs Region loved the isolation of a country highway; choosing when and where to stop, for how long and who to greet. Flying was about convenience and the Territory was about something far more important—personal freedom. But this time the trip between Alice Springs and Dunmarra was far from an enjoyable experience. As Col Hardman's immediate superior, it was Moore who had the final say in how to handle the search for Clinton Liebelt, and he had no choice now but to call off, or at least dramatically scale down, the search. It was more than a week since the boy had gone missing and the last whisper of hope that he was still alive out there had disappeared. In truth he had probably been dead for several days and it was only the incredible enthusiasm of the search teams that kept alive the notion of a miracle survival. In his two decades as a Territory officer, Dave Moore had never seen such a community reaction.

He had left Alice at 3 a.m. on Saturday, by himself behind the wheel as usual. Like his colleagues, Dave Moore was not a man for the pomp and ceremony of his rank. He preferred the camaraderie of the rank and file. That was why he'd left Adelaide in 1970 to pursue his police career up north, away from the city life which seemed to be bogged down in rules and regulations. But it made the Dunmarra search all the more difficult to handle. He had come up in the force with officers like Trevor Green and Col Hardman and knew how tough it would be to be involved in a search for a colleague's son. He also knew Steve Liebelt well. They'd worked together at Alice Springs when Steve first entered the force, after Moore had returned from a five-year posting at Kulgera where Steve would eventually follow. The parallels were endless and painful.

As he drove through the early morning, Moore reassessed the position. The major problem they faced was the number of volunteers who were still stopping to help. Many had literally jumped in their cars to drive there from all over the Territory; others had stepped off tourist buses in shorts and thongs, too caught up in the emotion to realise that their unprepared involvement was a liability rather than a help. It wasn't just the potential for injury that had Moore worried; the size of the search team was now seriously slowing its progress. He and Hardman had to somehow stem the tide without damaging the enormous sense of community spirit that had evolved. The compromise would be to pare back the search team to a combination of task force, local police and the cattle station people who knew what they were doing. The other volunteers would have to be sent home. Privately he also had concerns for his own men. They were a tough bunch physically—could march all day in this heat and terrain—but sooner or later the emotion would catch up with them. This was already obvious in many of the volunteers.

Moore had made a fleeting visit to Dunmarra the day Col Hardman arrived to take command. He wanted to keep it low-key but ensure that his former task force deputy knew he had the full support of senior command. The level of activity that day had amazed him, but it was even more astounding to see that it had not dropped off five days later.

As he and Hardman walked slowly from the dining room command centre toward the Liebelt house, Moore rehearsed what he wanted to say to Steve and Adele. He knew that Hardman's job had been made more difficult not just because he knew Steve personally but because the search had operated from the roadhouse. He and the Liebelts were thus forced to confront each other each day about the ebb and flow of the search; the Liebelts wanting information and Hardman simply unable to provide it. Moore wanted to choose his words carefully, to appeal to Steve as a former copper, someone who knew the realities of these operations and their side issues, like the number of people going down each day from heatstroke. The last thing you wanted to do was endanger the lives of people searching.

Adele watched the pair approaching from the kitchen window, and knew what was about to happen. It was a strange feeling; for the first time in a week she felt more resolute than anxious, almost calm, as Dave Moore told them that the formal search would end today. It was no surprise; it had to happen. If anything she felt sorry for Col Hardman because it was a bloody tough job, particularly as he was dealing with the child of a former colleague, part of the brotherhood. Not only would he have to leave without finding Clint, he also had to shoulder responsibility for the decision to call it off. She wanted to tell him that this was not the finish for the family, just a realisation that Clinton was gone. They still needed to find his body but she understood why the search had to end. Steve nodded quietly.

Outside, Dave Moore broke the news to the waiting media. If anything the weather was getting worse and somebody had to draw a line in the sand. Sunday would be the last day of the official search. After that the line searches, which still involved over 200 people each day, would be abandoned: 'I have a responsibility to ensure the welfare and safety of all persons within the search area and that cannot be ensured under the present conditions.'

24
It's only the helmet...

The campsite began stirring before sun-up on Monday as people started preparations to pull out of Dunmarra. Their progress was slow, not because of the complexity of rolling up swags and packing haversacks, but because of their reluctance to leave with the search unresolved. Steve Liebelt stood to one side watching the activity and reflecting on the emotional speech he had delivered in the roadhouse dining room the previous night. This debriefing would be the last, Col Hardman had announced after dinner. As reluctant as he was to call a halt, the search was now formally over and he would be pulling his men out the following morning. Though he understood the trauma this would cause to many of them, the search had to end at some stage. They had found nothing of substance in the past three days and the manpower and equipment needed to further extend the search could not be justified. The army had already gone and the NTES was leaving.

The room was quiet when Hardman finished. Until that moment no-one had considered the awful possibility that Clinton might never be found, only that he would be alive or dead. Steve stepped forward into the silence. He was a man who filled any room with his size but the awe in which he was held at this moment was a reflection of his resilience and leadership, not his physical strength.

They were the hardest words he had ever spoken: 'It's been nine days now since Clint disappeared and yet there are still hundreds of you here searching for a boy that some of you never even knew. As much as we would all like to think there is still hope I want you to know that, like all of you, I accept the truth that Clint has not made it. The police have made the only decision they could. It was inevitable that the search would have to end. Don't consider that what has been done here has been a failure. It has been a triumph of people and spirit. Adele and I can never thank you enough for what you have done, but it is now time to go home and get on with your lives. You too have families and they need you now.'

Steve paused there, trying to hold his emotions in check before the hushed crowd. When they finally came, the words were quiet but steely in their resolve: 'I want you to know that this will not stop me from searching. I can't and won't stop until I find my boy.' The whole room bent their heads and sobbed.

It seemed now, the morning after the search had officially ended, that there were as many determined to stay, preparing themselves for another day in the bush, as there were those who had to leave. A ground search team was already in the bush on a grid line and at least 19 men and horses, under the direction of Rob Teague and Noely Campbell, had left the roadhouse before daylight to search even further west. What would drive these people, many of whom Steve had not even met, to push themselves physically and emotionally in a search for a child obviously already dead? Steve thought about those who desperately wanted to stay but couldn't. Trevor Green had wept the night before after being ordered back to Darwin. He had left, arguing to the last minute with his superiors, who had decided enough was enough, and vowing to return at the end of the week. Steve had never seen the tough bloke cry before, and the sight was unsettling. He knew that Trevor's emotion was not just about the death of Clinton. It was about his own sense of failure that the boy had not been found. They all felt it.

There was no need to rush this morning. It was better to take the time and assess what resources were left and how best to use them. Peter Kerr had already left with the team of ringers. They had gone just after 4 a.m., riding slowly out to the Buchanan Highway to the last search point established by the army almost four kilometres further west of the official search site. Their plan was to ride about 10 kilometres into the scrub from the road and reach a fence line where the horses would be rested and watered before riding back out. Steve was planning to head out on one of the motorbikes, maybe after an early lunch. As he wandered back toward the roadhouse, trying to focus on what lay

It's only the helmet…

ahead, Col Hardman came out the door: 'They've found the helmet. The ringers have found it.'

Scott Fraser, a 17-year-old stockman from Humbert River station, had found the helmet. Scott didn't know the Liebelts, and yet he had made the 500-kilometre round trip along the unsealed Buchanan Highway to Dunmarra not once but three times in the past week for no reason other than that he wanted to help a neighbour in trouble. Scott had been one of the first to arrive the previous Sunday with Rob Teague. He joined the search team the following day, then drove back to Humbert River to do a bore run, immediately heading back to Dunmarra when he'd finished it to arrive just after 1 a.m. on Wednesday. That afternoon he joined the grid search before again heading back to the station until Saturday afternoon, when he was recalled to Dunmarra as part of the horseback search team.

He would later recount the discovery in a statement to police:

> We left Dunmarra and travelled out along the Buchanan Highway for approximately 13.5 kilometres. At this spot the horses were unloaded and we mounted up and commenced a line search in a southerly direction on a compass bearing of 146. We travelled for nine kilometres and then we all moved across to the west and commenced another line search in a northerly direction back on a bearing of 326 to the Buchanan Highway. Approximately five kilometres from where we turned around I was riding through some very thick turpentine scrub when I saw something white shine in the sun. I yelled out for the rest of the line to stop as they were about five to 10 metres in front of me. One of the other riders rode over to the helmet and said: 'It's only the helmet, there's no body here.'

Rob Teague moved his horsemen away from the scene and called over Noely Campbell, who squatted in quiet reverence as he studied the scene in minute detail. The helmet was full of spear grass, collected as Clinton carried or dragged it with him through the bush by the chin strap. He had walked out of the bush from the south-east and collapsed, exhausted, in a clump of spinifex. The crushed stalks showed he must have lain asleep for some time, curled in a foetal position around his security blanket—the helmet. There were also signs that he had woken, climbing out of the spinifex and walking north, the helmet now forgotten in his stupor. The tracks—the faintest of impressions in the concrete-like surface, disappeared almost immediately in heavy grass. Rob decided to wait until Steve Liebelt had been flown out to confirm it was Clinton's helmet before regrouping. He made the call that so many had been waiting to hear: 'Tracker One here...we've found the helmet... repeat, we've found the helmet...do you understand? Over.'

Steve was in a helicopter piloted by Steve Stanley—the only one left at Dunmarra—with Darwin policeman Dennis Field within minutes of Rob Teague's call, his heart in his mouth as they flashed over the scrub toward the site. Thoughts tumbled through his mind. All week they had been finding bits of clothing scattered over a dozen kilometres, as Clinton shed them in his distress. But Steve knew he wouldn't have let go of the helmet—not until he didn't have the strength left to keep going. It was his security. Clinton had to be nearby. Was there a chance he was still alive? Of course not. God, he hoped there was a body to be found. God, he hoped it was not too terrible. The five-minute helicopter trip seemed like an hour. How far had Clinton travelled? The helmet was miles further out than anyone had thought was possible. As they hovered above the scene the stockmen and their horses were almost impossible to spot beneath the canopy of the bullwaddy scrub. And he could see why no-one had been able to spot the white helmet from the air. It had fallen upside down, black padding facing the sky.

Rob Teague organised his men while Steve identified the helmet as his son's. They were close now—they could all sense an end to the nightmare—so it was more important than ever to keep the line tight and straight. Noely Campbell, the one man he could trust to ride in a straight line through the tangled scrub, was the last rider on the left. The others, just 20 metres apart, would take their reference from him. They moved off slowly, heading north. Behind them Steve and Dennis got back in the chopper with Steve Stanley, believing they might be able to spot the body from above. Steve could not contain his emotions any more. He put his hands in his head and sobbed; great heavy gasps from a man who had held so much inside for so long. It was a flood; a tirade against himself. Everything hurt. Here he was crying when he was supposed to be looking for his son. How could he be so weak at a time he was supposed to be so strong?

Steve could see the horsemen moving slowly back toward the Buchanan Highway. The chopper moved to the other side of the grid line, trying to cover as much area as possible. Still nothing. They had found all his clothing now, except the shirt he was wearing. There was nothing else to focus on except the hope that his body was in the open and not under a tree where it could not be seen. Even though he knew they were close, the task still seemed hopeless. Steve looked back at the horsemen, now a kilometre away to the west. The line looked broken. Something had happened. Steve Stanley turned in his seat. He had just taken a radio call from the ground crew: 'Steve, they've found him.'

Barry Grove, riding in the middle of the line, had moved barely 200 metres from the helmet when he spotted something out of the corner of his eye. It looked like a knee sticking out of the grass just to his right. He called a halt and quickly moved forward. It was Clinton's body, stretched out, as if asleep, next to a log among a ring of gums. The search was over.

25
We'll finish with some water as you go

Rob Teague cleared the scene around the body, ordering everyone but Barry Grove and Ted Hart out of eyesight. Struggling with his own emotions, he forced himself to look at Clinton—a boy he had never met. At least the poor kid was at peace now. The body had clearly been there for several days, dried out like a mummy and almost teak in colour. He grabbed a saddle blanket from one of his men and placed it gently over the body.

The helicopter was put down just 100 metres from the helmet. As Steve rushed half stumbling from the machine before the whirring blades had even stopped, he could see the stockmen and their horses standing quietly in a half circle in a small clearing beneath five little gums. Rob, Ted and Barry were crying quietly, holding their hats across their chests in respect. Steve walked to the trees and saw that someone had placed a saddle blanket over the body.

There was his little boy. He could see the long skinny feet, so big for his age yet so small now, dried out and a strange blacky-brown colour. There were cuts all over the legs where he'd been slashed by grass and branches as he ran blindly through the bush, not knowing where he was going or why no-one had found him. The wounds had long since dried up but ants, hundreds of them, were in there feeding as nature took its course. Steve sat down next to his son and gently pulled away the blanket. Clinton was dressed only in his underpants. At least he looked at peace, hands across his chest and eyes closed—asleep, with no fear of the darkness anymore. Steve checked under his eyelids; the eyes were still there and were still blue, thank God. He tried holding one hand but it was dry and lifeless, like holding an old stick. He cast his eyes slowly down the body, assessing the wounds, which seemed superficial, even a bruise across his ribcage where he'd obviously run into a tree. Still, it was enough for the dirty ants to get into his belly. Instinctively Steve tried to cuddle his boy but the body was rigid and unyielding. He lost control, crying and screaming. The others gently prised him loose and half carried him from the scene. Steve couldn't stand by himself. He just wanted to be with Clinton; to lie down beside him and hold him even though it was too late.

※ ※ ※

Peter Kerr strained forward in his seat as if the silent urging could somehow push the helicopter, flown by Steve Stanley who had returned to the roadhouse, faster toward its destination. He couldn't speed it up, just as he wasn't able to change the devastating situation he and Tom Williams were about to confront. Clinton had been found. The child was long dead and the condition of his body could be horrendous; invaded by insects, shrunken by the sun or even torn apart by animals. He grimaced at the thought. Steve Liebelt was already at the scene and Peter could only imagine his distress. The emotion of the discovery had been washed away by the adrenalin rush of needing to reach his friend to fulfil a promise to be there at his side when Clinton's body was found.

It had been Steve's request a couple of nights before, as they sat talking in Clinton's room long after most of the search crew had gone to bed. Steve had known the search, now into its second week, was about to be scaled down. He wasn't angry; he knew it was the right decision, but it didn't soften the reality of the moment when all hope would be officially declared lost. He could only think of how to keep going when everyone else had gone: 'I've got to find a way to keep looking, raise a bit of money from somewhere to buy radios, tents and anything else we need to keep going out there. I just want to know who'll stay with me till we find him.'

Peter hadn't hesitated: 'You don't need to ask. I'm staying till it's over, but why don't we start using the ringers a bit better. We've got 50 of 'em out there and they can all ride if you get the stations to send horses and feed. They can cover more distance and see more because they're higher in the saddle.'

Steve had supported the idea when they went to see Col Hardman the next day. Until then, Hardman had been reluctant to allow anyone but the army to operate outside the official search grid. It weakened resources and would be devastating if they ultimately missed the body. But he could not deny the sense of the suggestion now, as the search was being wound back, provided that Peter Kerr organised the horses and feed. Within a day he had arranged a rotation of animals and stockmen from the surrounding properties.

This fateful morning they had made one pass into the bush before Peter met them with supplies just after 10 a.m. Returning to Dunmarra in the four-wheel-drive for more water and feed, he was just a kilometre from the roadhouse when he saw the helicopter take off. Somehow he knew as he watched the dust explode around it that something dramatic had just happened. It was the moment they had been both waiting for and dreading. Hardman confirmed the discovery of the helmet as he pulled in.

As the chopper hovered above the clearing, Peter's worst fears were realised. He could barely make out the horsemen beneath the scrub but he could see Steve, swaying back and forth with his hands around a gum tree, screaming his anguish to the heavens. The others were giving him a wide berth, but Peter hurried to Steve's side as he collapsed, the broken trunk still in his hands. He was spent, a failure in his own mind because he couldn't find his son until it was too late.

Tom Williams bent down beside them. 'Steve, you've got to get up. We have to anoint the body. You have to talk to Clinton.'

It wasn't an order but encouragement to get up and keep going. It was something that Steve knew he had to do, if he could find the strength. Peter and Tom took an arm each and walked him to the side of the body. As they approached, past the group of horsemen silently watching, Peter was relieved to see that somebody had put a saddle blanket over Clinton's remains. He could just make out the boy's fingertips but the rest, whatever was there, had been covered.

Tom Williams decided otherwise. He wanted Steve to face Clinton again. Nothing less would do. He reached down and raised the blanket.

To Peter's relief he could tell it was his godson. His body had dehydrated but apart from the ravages of the bush on the soles of his feet, and a gash on his shoulder where he'd run into a tree, the body was whole. Clinton looked as if he'd lain down beside the log, gone to sleep and never woken up again.

Tom Williams broke the silence. Struggling with his own emotions, he could see the stockmen and police standing back to give Steve some room. Something had to happen; he had to find a practical way to perform some form of last rites over the body. Tom took off his army hat, filled it with water from his canteen and handed it to Steve, then gently anointed the body: 'We thank God that we finally found you, Clinton, just as we thank God for the family that loves you. Clinton, this is the stuff you died without but we'll finish with some water as you go to God.'

It was one of those moments—the toughest day of his life—when Tom knew that his decision to become a priest had been the right one. He could feel God's presence in the bush grove as he turned to Steve: 'Now talk to him Steve. Tell Clinton that you've found him.'

Steve nodded and knelt beside his son. He began speaking softly: 'I'm sorry Clint. We couldn't get there on time. Daddy let you down but I'm here now. I've come to take you home to Mum.'

When he stood up Peter could see that his mate had found some sort of peace. He had achieved something worthwhile in confronting his worst fears and being able to say goodbye, as a man. The saddle blanket was placed back over the body and Steve was walked away from the scene. It was time to leave; let others take care of the body which would be flown to Darwin for autopsy and official confirmation of his terrible death.

Nothing much was said on the way back to the roadhouse—even though it was almost impossible to talk above the roar of the helicopter, there was really nothing to say. They landed to the north of the roadhouse, away from the crowds now clustered near the campsite where the choppers normally landed. Peter didn't want Steve to have to walk past so many people to reach his family.

Adele was waiting by the gate. She had been told only minutes before that her son had been found and was feeling a strange mixture of relief that the search was finally over, grief that her darling son was dead and anger that others had made a decision that she should not see the body.

Adele knew the men had meant well. She had overheard the police discussing the condition of the body, expressing surprise that there were no birds in the area. They had stopped in dismay as she walked into the room, demanding to know what they meant. The question hung in the air, unanswered, as she realised that birds of prey would normally feast on anything dead. It meant that Clinton's body had not been touched by birds, nor torn apart by wild animals. It seemed the Aboriginal women and their spirits had indeed been protecting Clinton as they had promised.

Early on in the search Adele had prepared herself to go to Clinton as soon as he was found, no matter how bad his condition, but she could not be sure that she would have gone today. What upset her was that she had not been given the choice. Unlike Steve, whose grief had exploded spontaneously at the sight of his son's body, there was no visual trigger for Adele; just the words and tears of others. At the funeral several days later Adele would look at the little coffin and wonder how she would ever be certain that Clinton's body was really inside or whether this was just a ruse to end everyone's pain. The regret would last for years.

26
Clint is home

Night finally wrapped Dunmarra and its sadness in a cocoon of velvet. For the first time in a week the ebb of daylight was a welcome relief rather than yet another frustration. Clinton Liebelt had been found. Their task was over but the dozens who remained still wanted Steve and Adele to tell them it was time to leave. Finally Steve strode into the roadhouse, acknowledging those who quietly offered their condolences before disappearing into the storeroom behind the bar where he began pulling out flagons of rum and rows of plastic cups.

'I think we all deserve this,' he announced, standing on a chair, Peter Kerr at his side in case the emotion of the moment overcame him. 'You people will never know the gratitude Adele and I feel for coming out and helping to search. We have witnessed human nature at its best. The search is over. Clinton is home. Thank you all.'

They drank in relief, a giant group therapy session in which tears and laughter combined to open the floodgates of emotion stored up for the past nine days. Most had cried at some stage during the search, some many times. This was a wake of sorts; not so much a celebration of Clinton's existence but an acknowledgment of their own deeds, that life in the outback was treated with respect and its citizens responded in a time of crisis the way it should.

The task force police and ringers stood together, an unlikely group before the search but now bonded in their dust and dried sweat. As the night wore on and the alcohol took its effect, one of the officers sought out Peter Kerr and asked if he could souvenir one of the ringer's boots: 'I'd always thought that people in the bush were hiding from something or someone; that they were insecure and just wanting to get out of society, but I now realise that it's not the case. We're trained for this stuff and we've got equipment designed to keep us on our feet all day, but these blokes aren't and they've stayed with us all week. They're as tough as they come, and they've got our respect.'

Peter Kerr watched as Steve had a couple of drinks while circulating the room to thank people individually, and then disappeared quietly. He wondered how his mate would cope after everyone left and life returned to some semblance of normality, not that things would ever be normal again. They had assumed Steve would be okay during the search; that his experience as a copper would be enough to help him keep going. It had, but only on the surface. Peter could tell that there were a lot of emotions boiling inside his head. Only time would tell what scars would not heal.

Allen Eade had been in the roadhouse classroom finishing an on-air lesson with Greg and the other children that morning when Adele and Val Brooks walked in. He knew immediately from their grim demeanour that Clinton's body had been found. Nothing was said as they beckoned Greg from the room to join the rest of the family. Now, as he nursed a beer and talked quietly with eight of his colleagues who'd joined him on the search, Allen wrestled with his emotions. The classroom had felt like a prison in the last few days; he'd felt trapped inside the air-conditioned walls knowing that others far less able physically were out there in the heat. Knowing the reasons why didn't make it any easier to cope. He thought about the other kids in the Buchanan cluster. Clinton's classmates didn't see each other often but it didn't mean they weren't close, especially when Clinton was such a vibrant and dominant personality in the classroom or on the sports field. Kids were resilient but it would take some time for them to come to terms with what had happened.

Andy McLay was finding it more difficult than most to come to terms with Clinton's death. He often thought about his own impending demise, wondering how the debilitations of muscular dystrophy would hasten it, and the death of someone as young and healthy as Clinton made him as angry as it made him sad. The last time he had seen his little mate was the day before he disappeared. They'd had an arm-wrestle in the bar; Clint had won, as usual.

Andy wasn't a religious man but his views of the church had been softened since the search, changed by the man sitting next to him at the bar, the Reverend Tom Williams. Andy had watched him during the week, drifting among the crowd of exhausted searchers as they returned each night, helping them talk about their experiences. Andy liked his rough and ready style; sympathy and understanding laced with a cold beer and a sharp sense of humour. He decided that if anyone was going to speak over his coffin it would be Tom Williams. But he was still angry that God could allow Clinton to die in such a way. 'You know Tom, when I die I'm going to go up to the Pearly Gates, knock on the door and punch Saint Peter in the gob when he comes out. Then I'll come back down here. Bugger them.'

Tom nodded and smiled grimly. He knew that many others would feel the same way—that Clinton's death was an injustice. It was the sort of tragedy which would test the belief of any Christian. He had witnessed death many times over the years, even dealt with the tragedy of cot death, but nothing could compare with what had happened today. It was the tension of the search that made it different; the fact they had been searching for so long. And then to stand viewing the body, not in the confines of a funeral parlour or a church surrounded by family but in the middle of the boiling bush, alone with the boy's father—it was a physical and psychological isolation that he hoped would never be repeated. 'People found it nerve-racking,' he would write later in his monthly newsletter. 'A lot suppressed their normal response systems to prolonged trauma and stress. I think it reminded people too of their own mortality where one moment everything's right and God's in his heaven and all's well in the world, and then all of a sudden life can be such a short span.'

Steve hung around long enough for a couple of drinks before heading to the house in the hope that he might sleep to blanket the pain. Adele stayed on, feeling that one of them needed to be there with the people who had helped them. She and the girls were amusing themselves to keep the tears at bay. Their silly schoolgirl game of watching the task force officers getting changed in the office spilled over into their farewells; each of them lining up several times to get an extra round of hugs from the strong and willing young men. Patricia Stokes joined in until her husband jokingly asked if she wanted a 'taskie' for Christmas.

Despite the attempts at fun, Patricia couldn't shake her feeling of devastation. She had watched in awe and admiration as Steve made his short speech just hours after finding his son and wondered what strengths her son-in-law possessed to be able to stand up at such a moment and hold his composure. From the moment Dr Brooks had put Adele to sleep with tranquillisers on Wednesday, after she had asked that Patricia go to Clinton if they found him while she slept, she'd known that her grandson was probably dead. The doctor had turned and quietly told her there would be no room for her in the helicopter if they found Clinton. 'They'll be too busy working on him,' he said, his hand resting gently on her shoulder.

Instead, she channelled her energies into her daughter, shadowing her every move until she collapsed into bed herself for a few hours of disturbed sleep. She couldn't eat and had to force herself to drink, thinking of Clinton out there without water for days.

She looked at the piece of paper in her hand, the one handed out by the counsellors to warn people about the signs of trauma which were likely to follow in the days, weeks and even years ahead. Loss of memory was one of them, and she couldn't remember a damn thing. Everything piled up so that nothing made sense. She was not alone. One wit had asked her if she wanted to attend a meeting of the CRAFT Club—the 'can't remember a fucking thing' club.

Patricia thought of the support they'd received from people they didn't know and might never meet again, in particular the time she and Adele were in the tent chapel at one of the evening services. Adele was sitting on the floor with her head in her mother's lap. They were alone apart from Mike Ellemor who was speaking quietly at the makeshift altar. Patricia realised that a young woman had entered quietly and was kneeling behind them. She wore glasses and was dressed in the khaki of the army. She had come in to pray with them. The next morning as she helped serve breakfast Patricia saw the same young woman and thanked her for her support. 'I will never forget you,' Patricia told her. When they buried Clinton five days later Patricia would notice just two faces out of the sea of mourners; that of a young Aboriginal boy who ran across the street to place a flower on the coffin and that of the same young army woman who was handing out pamphlets as they arrived at the church. But she would never know her name.

When the ABC rang later in the evening to check reports that Clinton's body had been found Greg answered the phone.

'What's all the noise?' the reporter asked the boy.

'Oh, they're just having a party,' Greg replied nonchalantly.

Dave and Sandy Langan were not among those inside the roadhouse. They had slipped away unnoticed as the crowd milled around waiting for Steve and Adele. It was now 11 days since Phoenix had run off, igniting a sequence of events that would forever change their lives. The Langans' arrival at Dunmarra had not been the cause of the tragedy, merely an innocent trigger. So many other factors had combined to cause the boy's disappearance. When they drove away with the horses, they were still unaware that Clinton was not even supposed to have been at Dunmarra that day.

The Langans had been unable to speak to Adele or Steve in the hours after Clinton's discovery. It was a blessing because neither would have known what to say. A few weeks later Sandy would pen an awkward letter of thanks to the Liebelts:

> I really don't know how to start this letter. I just felt I wanted to write to you as we never got the chance to see you or speak to you when we had to leave.
>
> I want to thank you for your understanding, kindness and generosity when we arrived at Dunmarra. It only took us a very short time to realise that you were genuine, caring people.
>
> I will never forget any of you and hope it is of some comfort that you know we are thinking of you. If it is okay I would like to send some photos of the horses up to Greg later.
>
> I will never, never forget Clinton.

27
A renewed faith in human kindness

The assessments and plaudits came swiftly as the Northern Territory prepared for one of the biggest and most poignant funerals in its history. The search for Clinton Liebelt had left an indelible mark—good and bad—on a community which over the years had seen more of its share of upheaval and devastation—from events such as Cyclone Tracey and the loss of Azaria Chamberlain.

The time for stoic resolution was now past for Col Hardman, who broke down during one television interview—a rare moment when emotion finally got to the seasoned officer: 'The search has touched every person involved. We've had searches for people lost in the bush before, but never with the same community reaction. Everyone who came within cooee of the place offered to help. We had to knock some back just to be able to control the situation. Obviously people reacted because it was a child who was lost, and everyone can relate to the helplessness of a child.'

Hardman defended the search strategy, said everything had been done to find Clinton: 'We did our best. The problem with a search like that is that you are always behind the person, trying to catch up. The trackers were important to us from the very beginning because we wanted to be able to predict in which direction he was going so we could get in front of him. Unfortunately, it appears he was already past us. The ground was so hard out there that it made it impossible to follow tracks for more than a few metres. To have travelled that far without shoes on is really quite remarkable. It does surprise me. Of course, we don't know how long it took him to cover the distance. He may have done it in a couple of days in a panic.'

The most difficult thing to accept was Clinton's death: 'I think the fact we're dealing with a child makes it more difficult. Many people suffer from guilt, from the feeling that they could have done more, that they are somehow responsible. Everyone wanted to find him alive, and when that looked improbable we wanted to make sure we found the body. I think that even before we found him the family had already come to terms with the fact that Clinton had probably died. It's been important for them to clear it up in their minds as to where he was, and so they can put the boy to rest.'

When she decided in the middle of the week that her grandson had died, Patricia Stokes kept a notebook in her pocket to ensure she remembered the hundreds who had come to help. Now she wanted to pass on her message of thanks, which was published in the local papers:

> Even though the end result has been one of heartbreak and tragedy...our faith in human nature has been restored by the hundreds of people who gave their time in the search, running the roadhouse and feeding the masses. Life will never be the same without our little Clint; he will remain in our hearts forever. But our lives have been touched by the comradeship, support and love so freely given by the people of the NT and beyond. Thank you for all your prayers and for the support, comfort and love we have received.

There would be no inquest. Instead, the Deputy Coroner of the Northern Territory, Ray Minahan, released a report which recounted in broad detail how the search was mounted and organised until its inevitable discovery and conclusion. His conclusion told the real story:

> Those who assisted in the search cannot be commended enough. The police for their co-ordination and supervision, the army and RAAF for their logistic and personnel support and, of course, the civilian volunteers, those from surrounding stations and people just passing through who assisted, and those who travelled to Dunmarra specifically to assist the search. They all volunteered

their time to take part in a search in an area of extremely inhospitable terrain and weather conditions. Society in general, I feel, would commend them all.

Adele finally decided it was time to talk publicly, granting one interview which she conducted sitting in the cluttered office of the roadhouse. For the three hours she spoke, Adele never took her eyes off the west, staring out past the petrol bowsers into the land where Clinton had been lost. 'We had to find him,' she sighed. 'I just couldn't stand having to look out from the shop across into that bush every day knowing he was out there somewhere.'

It was a resigned acknowledgment that some measure of relief had been achieved from the tragic yet inspiring search for her son—tragic because a young boy had suffered a lonely death, inspiring because it united a far-flung and hard-bitten community in a common cause.

The death of Clinton Liebelt was seen by many as heroic—an odd epitaph for a boy who was pitted unfairly against the unforgiving nature of one of the most isolated places on earth, and lost. In the horrible reality of an unthinkable death, some had found a reason to be in awe of its victim; wondering how a small boy managed to travel such a distance over such terrain.

Barefoot, almost naked and hallucinating from dehydration, Clinton travelled 23 kilometres measured in a straight line (and who knows how much further as he wandered west in circles), in searing heat, before he finally, and mercifully, succumbed. But the real truth of character, or heroism, in the tragedy was the spirit of a community—and it was that to which Adele and Steve Liebelt would always cling.

'Clinton has renewed our faith in human kindness,' Adele said. 'Everyone is put on this earth for a reason, and I believe Clinton's task was to bring the people of the Northern Territory together. I don't consider myself a religious person—I can't remember the last time I went to church—but I prayed an awful lot during that week.'

✷ ✷ ✷

There were never going to be enough places inside the Uniting Church at Katherine for the sea of mourners. Like the desperate search for his life a week before, Clinton Liebelt's funeral evoked emotion on a scale never before seen in the Territory. The louvres which lined the walls of a structure that normally housed a few dozen parishioners each Sunday were flung open as more than 400 spilled into the grounds outside. They massed in the swirling, musty heat for the obvious reasons, of sadness and support, but also because Clinton's death underlined the fragile nature of their own existence in this most remote of places. This was a funeral with no casual observers. They were all participants in his life. Most still fought vainly to find answers, not just why they couldn't find Clinton in time to save him, but why it happened at all. The question would remain unanswered forever.

Mike Ellemor, who took the service with Tom Williams, advised them not to try. He had been an intimate witness in the hours immediately after Clinton's body was found, first sitting with Adele in the emptiness while she waited for Steve to come back from the bush and then helping the family with their prayers. The experience had rocked him, and he had no answers either. He recalled a classroom debate years before when he was training to be a minister when they'd discussed the same question. The advice was that if he did not have an answer then it was better to say so.

'I remember a Sunday school teacher in Darwin many years ago who had served as an army nurse. She told us about people who had died and on the identifying documentation the letters GOK often were written in answer to questions like "Who is this person?" and "What happened to this person?" The answer code GOK stood for "God only knows".

'Why did Clinton go out there? Why didn't he keep by the bike? Why did he get lost? Why did he die? We are all asking why and I guess one of the reasons is because the person who has died is one that was so young. And it doesn't seem right to us when someone dies as a child. The answers elude us and I believe it would be dangerous of me to attempt an answer. There isn't any one answer to the question of why.

'Clinton has been, for us, a living gift from God. Just as plants sometimes die prematurely yet still can be called living gifts that keep on growing, so it is with Clinton.

'Already we are seeing many ways in which the search for Clinton has brought out so much good in people throughout the Territory and beyond. Already we are realising that in life and in death Clinton has affected us and affected our lives in ways that we will never forget.'

Almost 1200 kilometres to the south, the Reverend Doug Turnbull was reaching the same conclusion as he conducted a simultaneous memorial service for hundreds more who flocked to the John Flynn Memorial Church in Alice Springs: 'If the Christian conviction about death means anything, it means that those of us left behind are the ones to be pitied; especially Steve and Adele, whose hearts must be breaking, longing to see their little boy again. I, for one, am convinced that if Clinton could speak to us from the place where he has gone, he would tell us not to weep for him. Yes, weep for ourselves in our pain and our sadness and our confusion. Weep for his Mum and his Dad, for his brother, surround them with our love, write to them, ring them, tell them we care and feel for them. But don't weep for me, says Clinton; I've found my new home, the home to which I would one day have had to make the journey anyway. And if his competitive little nature came to the fore he might add, and ha, ha, I beat you home.'

Steve Liebelt's eulogy to his son did not dwell on his death but reflected on his achievements in life: 'Clinton typified the boy from the bush. Though only eight years of age he displayed a maturity at times which belied his age. People who knew him well knew of his passion for adventure, his abundant amounts of energy and his consummate desire to learn more about everything all of the time. His cheeky smile, mischievous antics, quick wit and loving nature endeared him to all those who were touched by him. He is remembered as the inquisitive know-it-all. The Professor, as he was referred to at times, knew it all and was not slow in saying, yeah, I know. Clinton always displayed a love of the country. He loved country people and country music. Garth Brooks was his idol. He takes Garth's music with him. His competitiveness in the schoolroom and sporting arena made him the envy of many of his friends. He had a tireless desire to be the best. Now Clint, you rest in peace with the God and Jesus you loved so much. You will never be far from us. You have brought peace and happiness to so many people. Few people are able to do this. You have brought so much faith back in mankind. Dad's Possum and Mum's Clintypops, rest in peace. You are with us forever.'

As they sat in their car outside the church waiting to follow the hearse, Steve and Adele stared in disbelief at the parade of flowers and people which poured from the building. It was like watching a movie at a drive-in, shielded behind the windscreen, while friends, family and strangers filed silently past. Adele broke the tension, unable to stop herself giggling at the sight of Reg Underwood, who emerged flapping his arms like a chook in a barnyard trying to cool his underarms in the heat. She felt guilty but couldn't help herself. A few minutes later she burst into tears as police directing traffic through town stood to attention and saluted as the hearse drove past on its way to the cemetery. Somehow everyone else beat them to the gravesite. The crowd seemed even larger now, rows and rows of them standing silently as Greg placed his brother's white helmet on top of the coffin before it was lowered into the earth. Inside the coffin was a leather folder filled with letters to Clinton from his School of the Air classmates.

By the time Steve and Adele got back to their room at the Katherine Hotel it was 8.30 p.m. There had been the ceremony at the cemetery and another at the School of the Air where a memorial garden to Clinton would soon be opened as the town found an outlet for its sadness. Despite the strains of the day they were hungry and wandered into the restaurant to eat before bed. The place was packed with mourners, and had run out of food. In an instant, arrangements were made for the town's Woolworth's store to be reopened to allow the hotel owners to put on a barbecue.

* * *

Just two weeks after Clinton's funeral, Dunmarra put aside its grief to host a mini-school for the Buchanan cluster of the Katherine School of the Air. Sixteen of Clinton's classmates and their parents made the journey to laugh, sing and play in the grounds where so recently there had been only tears.

Adele watched Greg running around the back paddock with his mates and wondered about his resilience. As much as she wanted to see Clinton out there she knew that life had to go on and the important thing now was to ensure that Greg would have as normal a life as possible.

Clinton had wanted answers to everything—how high, exactly, were the clouds, what would muscular dystrophy do to Andy McLay and why God, with all his power, couldn't or wouldn't stop people from dying. They were questions without answers to satisfy his expectations, just like the questions that followed his death. The only solace, indeed the only answers, had come from the response to his disappearance.

Among the 900 letters which poured in from across Australia and the rest of the world over the next few weeks, one stood out in particular. It was from Peter and Candy Kerr's daughter, Jacquie, born just two months after Clinton. Inside the envelope was a short note and $1.20 in change. It was Jacquie's pocket money, sent so Clinton could buy himself a cool drink on his way to Heaven.

Postscript

A decade has passed since Clinton Liebelt's death and for most of the people I interviewed as I attempted to reconstruct the search, the wounds are as fresh now as the day his body was found. But so are the memories of the amazing community response to a family in need—it remains one of the biggest manhunts in the history of a country renowned for its compassionate response to human crisis.

Steve and Adele's marriage did not survive the tragedy. At the time of writing, Steve still owns the Dunmarra Wayside Inn, where he lives with his new partner, Julie Meldrum. They have two young children. Ben Liebelt also lives and works at the roadhouse, as does Trevor Green, who quit the police force a few years ago and is now Steve's business partner. Adele married again but her new marriage lasted only briefly. She has now settled in Tennant Creek with her new partner, Alan Holland. Greg, now 21 years old, also lives in Tennant Creek. He and his partner, Becky Spence, are expecting their first child.

Adele has not crossed the Stuart Highway from the roadhouse since Clinton disappeared, but she does visit 'Clint's Place'—a memorial among the grove of trees where he died 23 kilometres north-west of Dunmarra. A track has been graded to the spot from the Buchanan Highway, just wide enough for a four-wheel-drive to pass safely among the clumps of lancewood and bullwaddy. There is a headstone, identical to another at the roadhouse and a third at the Katherine Cemetery, marking the place where Clinton lay down to sleep for the last time. To one side there is a small barbecue. The family comes here from time to time to remember their son, brother, nephew and grandson. Others come as well—people who remember not only the sadness of that week in October 1993 but its triumph of community spirit.

Notes on sources

I travelled to Dunmarra a few days after Clinton was found to interview Adele for the Sydney newspaper *The Daily Telegraph*. Until then she and Steve had refused all requests for interviews, nor had any photographs of the boy whose disappearance had captured the attention of media around the country been published. Adele's decision to talk to me was for no reason other than that I happened to contact her at the right time. I remember clearly the few hours I spent sitting in the office with her as she talked and stared out across the highway into the bush where Clinton was lost.

The story struck me immediately as one not only about a tragedy but also about a triumph of community spirit. The idea that a bunch of footballers would forfeit their match to drive 300 kilometres and spend the day searching the bush in searing heat was amazing, let alone the notion of the mini town which sprang up by the side of the highway during the search.

Nine years later, when I called her in Tennant Creek to ask about doing a book, Adele did not remember me. But she listened to my proposal and agreed to help, hoping it would finally give her closure on the search. 'Once I had read the book I could think of Clinton without ever having to think about the search again,' she told me. Steve, although initially hesitant, also gave the project his full support.

In reconstructing the events leading up to and including the search, I have relied mostly on interviews with the people involved. I also had access to the files held by the Northern Territory Coroner's Office and clippings of various media outlets which covered the search. Darwin historian Peter Forrest allowed me to use much of his research into the tales surrounding Noel and Ma Healey.

I have spoken to most of those named in the book. In particular I would thank the friends closest to Steve and Adele—people like Debbie Bruce, Peter Kerr, Trevor Green, Andy McLay and Val Brooks whose friendship provided the backbone of their support before, during and after the search. Others I spoke to included Pat Stokes, Greg Liebelt, Ben Liebelt, Alan Holland, Margie McLean, Allen Eade, Mike Ellemor, Tom Williams, Col Hardman, Dave Moore, Narda Morton, Candy Kerr, John and Val Dyer, Dave Langan, Sandi Mccue, Mark Robins, Steve Stanley, Greg Henckel, Richard Sallis, Rob Teague, Reg and Janelle Underwood, Damien Ryan, Jon Finn, Wes Binks, Aiden Burke, Andy Gray, Trevor and Chris Haines, Steve Twentyman and Peter Walkington.

The land west of Dunmarra—a bush hell where life and water are virtually non-existent.

Dusk at Dunmarra. The view past the windmills from the roadhouse. This is where Clinton rode his motorbike into the bush.

Peter Kerr was the picture of a Territory bushman: a lean, weathered face beneath a broad, sweat-stained hat, enjoying an ice-cold beer to wash away the day's toil.

The forecourt of the roadhouse became a parking lot each morning as busloads of townspeople from Katherine and other small communities arrived to help search.

Horses and stockmen were an integral part of the search for Clinton Liebelt. The animals were trucked in from properties across the length and breadth of the Northern Territory.

Mustering helicopters became a key search tool, covering enormous tracts of land while ground teams combed the bush below.

Volunteers from all walks of life were bussed into the bush each morning to begin the exhaustive line searches. At nightfall, many would return injured or sick.

Greg helps prepare breakfast. The search for his beloved brother was a psychological nightmare for the 10-year-old.

The 'Orange people'—Northern Territory Emergency Services volunteers—came to Dunmarra from dozens of towns to help search.

The roadhouse dining room was set up as the search command centre, where police and army personnel coordinated the activities of hundreds of searchers each day.

The kitchen at the Dunmarra roadhouse was manned around the clock to prepare meals and provisions each day for the searchers.

Volunteers in a line search at Dunmarra.

It was a solemn moment when Adele (left) visited Clinton's bush memorial a year after his death with Miss Val, Lu Stokes and Debbie Bruce.

The place where Clinton finally lay down and died—23 kilometres west of Dunmarra and far beyond the search lines. A saddle blanket marks where he 'lay down and went to sleep'.

THIS GARDEN IS NAMED
IN MEMORY OF
CLINTON LIEBELT
KATHERINE SCHOOL OF THE AIR STUDENT
AND WAS OFFICIALLY OPENED
BY
**POLICE SUPERINTENDENT
COLIN HARDMAN**
ON
1 DECEMBER 1993

A memorial garden to Clinton was established in the grounds of the Katherine School of the Air.